Overextended

A Practical Guide to Correcting the Housing Market

David M. Prentice

Common Sense

Legal Information Is Not Legal Advice

This book provides information about the law designed to help users safely cope with their own legal needs. But legal information is not the same as legal advice - the application of law to an individual's specific circumstances. Although measures have been taken to make sure the information is accurate and useful, I recommend you consult a lawyer if you want professional assurance that the information, and your interpretation of it, is appropriate to your particular situation. I, David Prentice, am not an attorney and in no way shall any information provided by me be considered legal advice.

Before Using Appendices

The Appendices of this book advise and present you with tools for your use in foreclosure defense. If you are using the Appendices you should read the following terms and conditions below. If you disagree with these terms and services, please do not use the Appendices section of this book.

I will never refer you to a specific attorney or service. You are solely responsible for making a selection of an attorney or other service.

I do not receive any portion of any legal fees charged by any lawyer. Similarly, I do not receive any portion of any subscription fees or royalties received from any of the recommend resources. Any fee arrangements are strictly between you and any attorneys, sites, or authors whose services you may or may not employ.

The release and security of any sensitive or confidential information transmitted by you to any attorney or service is your sole responsibility.

I do not endorse any particular attorney, legal service, or reference source and cannot guarantee the quality or reliability of any services provided by any of these resources.

Paperback ISBN: 978-0-9904215-0-4
Hardcover ISBN: 978-0-9904215-2-8
EBook ISBN: 978-0-9904215-1-1
Library of Congress ID: Pending (1-1448556101)

Common Sense

This book is dedicated to my father. You took a selfish, ignorant boy that took all in life for granted and transformed him into a man of real worth to the community. Thanks Dad.

ACKNOWLEDGMENTS

I dove into this venture thinking I'd need a little help here or there, but not much. It turns out that writing a book is easy… it's making it worth reading and getting it to people who want to read it that's tough. I almost gave up several times upon this realization. Nobody would have read a word I wrote if it wasn't for these tremendous people.

You probably wouldn't have cracked this book if wasn't for the fantastic cover created by Peter O'Connor. Thank you to my professional peers for copy-editing my poor excuse for English usage. Jason Anderson made sure my readers had a top quality reading experience, because if it weren't for him, this book would still be a word document. All of those who were so kind as to read, review, and provide input on my writing – I'm sure that was a difficult task; you've done a lot for me and I will not forget that. Ruth Mossok-Johnston, I appreciate your advice and pushing me to go for it and get this in print. JA Konrath, you too pushed me in that direction, all without ever knowing me – thank you for your work that I'm sure helps many others as well. Finally, I owe gratitude to Michael Sauvante for taking the time to educate me and review my work when he had absolutely nothing to gain and did not know me. I've quickly found that the writing community as a whole is a great one that truly supports its fellow contributors.

My support system has been nothing short of amazing. Few are as fortunate as I to have such amazing people in their lives to help them with any crazy project they dream up. In no particular order, my mom, my dad, my brothers James and Daniel, my dear friends Mike, Carl, Matt, Jasmina, and Jeff, my closest business associates Denny, Dean, and Keith, and of course, my girlfriend Allison have all been there for me throughout the project. I'm not an easy person to know, love, work with, or live with – all of you are exceptional and I love you. Thank you guys… you made a dream come true for me and helped to get important information to those in need of it.

CONTENTS

Introduction: Who am I and what is the purpose of this book?

I am not what most people would consider an expert. I'm not an economist, an attorney, a politician, or a financier. I don't have prestigious degrees from esteemed universities. And I believe that is exactly why this book is so important. While I have studied extensively, the majority of my knowledge of the housing market comes from professional and firsthand experience. This allows me to do what the experts have a very difficult time with – relate to everyday people like you.

Does presenting extensive statistical data with a hypothesized thesis really help anybody? It might help a professor escalate his career but aside from that the information is largely useless. I didn't spend countless hours writing to present a theory to a journal. Nor did I wish to utilize the experience I've accrued to teach people how to exploit homeowners for profit. If that's why you picked up this book, you might as well put it down. This book has a simple purpose: educate the average person about foreclosure and provide insight as to how to overcome it.

Contained within are some harsh realities, no doubt about it. We could all use a wake-up call and I did my best to provide that. Once we're on the same page, it's all about genuine solutions. I'm not here to be your friend and tell you that everything is fine. I'm here to inform you of the ways you can take control of your life to protect yourself and your loved ones. After you do that, we can be friends – and together we can help our nation as a whole correct this housing market crisis that has plagued us for too long.

Anybody that can read to this point and has a few hours to spare can learn and apply the lessons in this book. It took me eight re-writes and endless revisions to make sure of that. It turns out that I tend to fancy myself a scholar once I start writing; that didn't work too well. Instead I decided to chop it down to the essentials: how we got here, how foreclosure works, and how to overcome it. A resource section of various appendices was added to make it easy for those that wanted or needed more information. Simple and effective – the way it should be.

I'm happy with the final product you're holding. My only regret is that it took too long to get in your hands. Millions were affected before I could finally piece together what I wanted to teach people in a way that made sense. My family is included in that figure– my father received a foreclosure notice in late 2006. I remember being the first recipient of that news. As the eldest of five, my dad came to me to ask for help. I remember being almost paralyzed with anxiety, a feeling I'm sure you can relate to if you're reading this book.

At the time, I didn't know how to help. We learned together along the way and the battle lasted for over six years. During that time, my life transformed from sports and parties to a mission of helping as many people as I could. My father decided to move on with his life, having recovered financially. I assumed responsibility for my childhood home to test some legal theories we had. It made sense to use myself as a test dummy because I had nothing to lose.

I knew the arguments were right and lawful, but that didn't mean they would be effective. And they weren't. That home was ultimately lost to the bank. As is the case with most things in life, more was learned from that failure than any victory. Shame has since become pride as I use those lessons to help others be more successful than I was.

How did this horrible experience get transformed into a positive one? In 2011, Home Team was launched by my partners and I. Prior to that, I had worked for a local attorney as a case manager for almost two years. Home Team had but one purpose: protect homeowners from foreclosure using the legal system. A year later, we launched a sister company, Partners Recovery Solutions, to approach housing issues from a financial direction as well. Since then, my team and I have worked with all kinds of people to overcome their housing issues. The industry has evolved a lot in that time.

Here's the rub: despite all of that experience, I still can't just tell you exactly what you should do to fix foreclosure problems. I'm surrounded by attorneys, brokers, and investors that are all much smarter than me – they don't have the answer either. That's because there's no such thing as a "one size fits all" solution. Great, so this book is useless! Not exactly.

This short guide will inform you of exactly what to expect so you may prepare. It will give you options on how to counter foreclosure proceedings and guide you in reducing your options further to make the best choice for you. Necessary resources are provided to help you put that choice into action – all of the tools to complete the job are there. I don't believe it's enough to defend yourself; I think we each have a duty to help others as well. Therefore, the extra step was taken to explain how each of us has the power to invoke change on a broader scale.

It is my sincere hope that the information contained within prevents you or your loved ones from any harm. Don't stop there though. Plugging one hole in the hull of the ship is a great start. Your family matters and should be your first priority. Resurfacing the rest of the hull prevents the rest of the ship from sinking around you. I urge you to take that next step.

Part 1: How did it come to this?!

Foreclosure is an ugly word, invoking images of pained families and empty houses. The term 'housing market' doesn't fare much better our minds. It wasn't always this way – foreclosures used to be very rare and the housing market used to be held in a positive regard. Today foreclosure is an unfortunate part of everyday life. And the housing market has gone from eternally rising to a depressed state. Over the past 100 years there have been many key changes to our nation's fiscal policies, economics, and social trends. Too many of these have contributed to the deranged financial status we now dwell in.

I know that many of my readers will skip this part of the book and go straight to the more applicable chapters. I encourage you to take an hour from your day and learn this basic historical background of the foreclosure crisis. This is important because without understanding the history of the housing market, it's impossible to fully grasp the legal arguments presented later. The system surrounding foreclosure is a lot like any well-constructed lie: 80% truth (lawful actions) with 20% lie (fraud) mixed in. Most of the unscrupulous activities engaged in by lenders are legal if completed properly. Fortunately for banks, most people don't understand the strict rules they are required to follow that are designed to protect consumers and so they cut corners to earn greater profits. To cite an old cliché, knowledge is power. So please, take advantage of this easy to comprehend version of history on the topic so you can't be swindled due to ignorance.

At the start of the 20th century, most of our country's financial and housing concerns didn't exist or were miniscule in comparison to what we're experiencing today. As recently as 1913 there was no such thing as central banking in the U.S.; every dollar was backed by gold. There were no complex finance products. Buying a home was a very basic process – save up money and pay for it. Mortgages existed, but in a rudimentary sense. If you wanted a mortgage you had to put 50-80% of the amount as a down payment and then pay off the remainder within 5-7 years. Such a system ensured that nobody was overleveraged financially and people actually had a vested interest in their property. There was but one 'problem': less than half of people in the U.S. could afford to own homes and therefore rented. This problem has long since been solved (today about 68% of people own homes)[1] but at a tremendous cost.

On December 23, 1913, when most people were busy preparing for the holidays and blissfully ignorant of their political surroundings, the first and most significant step towards our current economic system was taken. Completing what could be considered his most regrettable act while in office as President, Woodrow Wilson signed the Federal Reserve Act creating the Federal Reserve System (or "Fed" for short). This new system was supposed to ensure that the U.S. would never again suffer banking panics as it had in the 1800s and early 1900s. It goes far beyond the scope of this book to discuss the intricacies of the Fed (Appendix G contains some suggested reading on the topic). In short, this non-government entity was given the power to adjust most aspects of our entire economy without oversight and is run by select individuals that are powerful in the banking industry.

The creation of the Fed marked the third time in history that a central bank was created for the United States. The first and second both resulted in massive debt and were allowed to die after their initial charters – we were not so fortunate this time. The Fed's purpose, as with all central banks, is to produce paper money in excess of the amount of actual value backing currency. It then controls the circulation and interest rates of that fiat money to banks across the nation. In theory this monetary system should lead to faster economic growth and more stability. In reality it keeps our nation in perpetual debt and devalues our currency with massive inflation.

One problem with the Fed is that the Federal Reserve Notes it outputs are intrinsically worthless, supported merely by "faith in the American dollar" because they have no assets backing them. Another is that fiscal policies are set for banks by bankers so therefore they look out for – you guessed it – bankers. The monetary system is unsound because the dollar value and monetary guidelines of our nation are subject to change on a whim. The bottom line is that without the Fed many of the current economic difficulties we face today (massive inflation, immense national debt, imprudent banking practices, etc.) could not exist.

It only took twenty years for the simplistic and effective financial structure that Americans had been reliant upon since our nation was founded to become completely unrecognizable. In 1933, under the guise of combating deflation, Franklin D. Roosevelt signed a bill that made it illegal to use gold as currency. Gold coins that were in public use had to be traded in for paper money. Those who resisted this new legislation were met with a fine of up to $10,000 and/or up to ten years in prison. The act also created a boost in Treasury reserves by setting a conversion rate of dollars to gold for citizens and then immediately raising that conversion rate by nearly 70%.[2] Apparently people weren't having a hard time already during the Great Depression; they had to be robbed by their own government as well. The theoretical objective of defeating deflation was achieved. Substantial inflation took its place then and thereafter. The paper notes originally issued by the Fed were backed by gold giving them real value. Unfortunately, this backing quickly went from 100% in 1913 to 0% in 1971[3] – an incredible feat for the banking industry but an absolute nightmare for the rest of us.

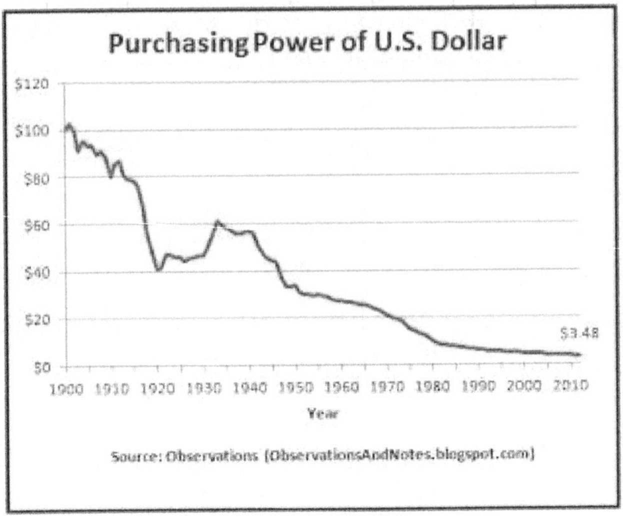

Quick Fact: $10,000 in 1933 is equivalent to $182,185 today.

Almost immediately after the transition to fiat currency, the Federal Housing Administration (FHA) was formed. With the FHA came mortgages similar to those we know today with low down payments and long periods to pay the loan back. At that time the industry standard became 15 years and then quickly jumped to 30 years, which is today's norm. Such risky lending scenarios were never offered previously because banks couldn't afford to have such large sums of capital lent out for such long periods of time. With the Fed only requiring them to reserve a fraction of their outstanding loans, they gained the necessary leverage to expand their lending capabilities. This made the profit and risk margins of these long-term loans acceptable.

There was a glimmer of fiscal conservatism during this fast-paced transformation of the financial sector in the form of the Glass-Steagall Act of 1933. The primary provision of this act mandated separation of commercial and investment banking. This meant that if a bank took deposits, it could not trade in anything but government bonds and if a bank underwrote securities, it couldn't take deposits. The reason for this was simple: banks were taking money from their depositors and putting those funds into high-risk investments to make a profit. Sometimes these failed and therefore lost a lot of money belonging to clients that had no involvement in the bank's transactions.

Congress decided to extend Glass-Steagall in 1956 by passing the Bank Holding Company Act (BHCA), barring commercial banks from engaging in non-banking activities, notably insurance. In doing so, they inadvertently presented the banking industry with an easily overlooked loophole. The BHCA stated specifically that it only applied to banks and defined banks as institutions that accept deposits and engage in commercial lending.[4] This led to the discovery of 'nonbank banks' which only do one or the other, thereby making them exempt from the rules that applied to banks. In later years, exploitation of this loophole would be critical in the undoing of regulatory legislation on financial institutions.

The government decided to get more intimately involved in the housing industry in 1968 with the establishment of the Government National Mortgage Association (Ginnie Mae). Ginnie Mae acts as a guarantor of loans for investors who purchase mortgages from loan originators. This is the equivalent of the government being a co-signer on mortgage loans for investors so they feel more comfortable buying loans from originators. Selling their loans equates to available capital for banks to lend more.

In 1970, Ginnie Mae set the stage for the rapid onset of the housing market issues we experience today with the advent of the mortgage backed security (MBS). Mortgage backed securities make sense in their fundamental form: take multiple loans from an originator and pool them together into one security which can then be purchased by an investor. This process saves both sides a lot of time and money from not having to handle each loan individually. Loans are supposed to be grouped together according to type and risk factor so that each "bundle" is easy to identify and price. These risk factors are determined by credit rating agencies and in theory if everything is factored out appropriately, there is no problem at all.

However, it doesn't take a rocket scientist to figure out "Hey, if we just throw a few bad eggs into the mix, we can get rid of those at the same price as the good ones and make more money". And that's exactly what began to happen over time – credit rating agencies were putting their AAA or A+

stamp on securities that contained a mix of both high and low risk loan products. Credit rating agencies are compensated by those who produce securities so it makes sense that they would be motivated to alter the ratings in their favor. Investors rely on the information provided to them from these agencies to make wise investment decisions. It wasn't until the bubble reached its pinnacle that those who bought the securities questioned anything. These days the credit rating agencies are under a lot of scrutiny because it was realized upon the bubble burst that their risk factors had been tampered with during the boom.

Jimmy Carter introduced two new acts in the early 1980s, allowing banks to merge and issue loans with adjustable interest rates. These laws made it possible to have a banking cartel whereby the biggest, strongest lenders in the nation could team up and combine resources. They could also control the market with the raising and lowering of loan interest rates. From then on lenders were pretty much free to create any type of loan products they wanted, leading to the conception of the many ludicrous mortgage types we have today including adjustable rate (and all of its options), interest-only, hybrid, and balloon mortgages, among others. These complex loan products are great for allowing people the ability to purchase homes with minimal up-front costs. They're not so great for people keeping those payments up as they can increase over time and sometimes the principal balance actually *rises* after each payment. It should come as no surprise that the vast majority of subprime loans and foreclosures stem from these newly developed mortgage types.

The Federal Reserve Board Chairman Paul Volcker was replaced by Alan Greenspan in 1987. The reasons behind the Chairman's termination were kept confidential, but some speculate that the Reagan administration had him removed from his position because he was not in favor of deregulation.[5] Shortly after the inception of Greenspan's reign, the Basal Accord was implemented which called for risk-based capital reserve requirements for banks. The structure for this policy had MBS tagged as low risk, therefore requiring low reserve requirements to back those products should they default. Banks definitely needed another excuse to leverage their capital further and originate more loans. During this same year, Wendy Gramm (wife of ex-Senator Phil Gramm) became the chairperson of the U.S. Commodities Futures Trading Commission. Mrs. Gramm was almost immediately successful in making derivatives and swaps exempt of any and all regulation. She repeated that feat in 1993 just before she resigned to take a seat on the board of Enron as a member of the audit committee.[67]

Continuing the trend, the Community Reinvestment Act, originally enacted in 1977, was modified by President Clinton to allow for enforcement capabilities. This legislation was originally passed for the supposed purpose of eliminating discrimination in lending. Now it gave banks set quotas for lending in distressed communities or they faced federal sanctions. It is now known that these loans defaulted at significantly higher rates than others which makes sense because they were intentionally pushed upon those unable to afford them.

An enormous merger took place in 1998 with Traveler's Insurance absorbing the lending branch of Citicorp to form Citigroup.[8] These were two of the nation's leaders in the banking and insurance industries. Those entities joining forces created a financial powerhouse, but the acquisition was in clear violation of the Glass-Steagall Act. However, if you recall the aforementioned BHCA, a tiny loophole for nonbanks was created and thus despite the violation the Federal Reserve granted Citigroup a temporary waiver for the joinder. This merger holds significance as the breaking point in regards to financial institution separation and deregulation.

You'll be shocked to hear that less than a year later the Gramm-Leach-Bliley Act (GLBA) was signed into law which removed those prohibited merger barriers. With the passage of the GLBA commercial banks, investment banks, securities firms, and insurance companies were allowed to consolidate under one roof and one individual could now be a member of multiple institutions. This legislation was primarily pushed into place by Senator Phil Gramm, backed by a $300 million fund from lobbyist and campaign contributors. Mr. Gramm was referred to as "the father of the foreclosure crisis" by Nobel Prize-winning economist Paul Krugman for his direct impact on this bill and several other policies. Other notable economists were quick to concur with that statement. It should be noted that federal records indicate that Gramm was the top recipient of campaign contributions from commercial banks and among the top five recipients of contributions from Wall Street corporations from 1989 until 2002 when he left the Senate and moved abroad.[9,10,11]

As we transitioned into a new millennium, the final piece of key legislation to lead us into the housing bubble was signed into law. The Commodity Futures Modernization Act exempted derivatives from regulation, supervision, trading on established exchanges, and capital reserve requirements. Any derivative (i.e. MBS) could now be traded in any manner with zero oversight. This immediately led to finance institutions deciding to "go all in" on the mortgage backed security boom. That same year the FBI issued a warning to the nation of an epidemic in mortgage fraud.[12]

Despite the entire legislative system leaning in favor of the financial institutions, a true housing boom couldn't take place without certain economic factors in a parallel state. That proved to be no issue as during the same time period the Fed decided to lower interest rates. Between 2001 and 2003 the Fed interest rate was lowered twelve times, from 6.5% all the way down to 1%, a historic low which couldn't possibly be maintained. It needn't be maintained long as the damage was done very quickly; mortgage originations nearly quadrupled in that time period.[13] The Fed apparently realized this could not work long term and from 2004 to 2006 the rate went back up 17 times to 5.25% before pausing. Astonishing as it may be, they saw fit to repeat the disastrous act and by 2008 the rate was back to one percent.

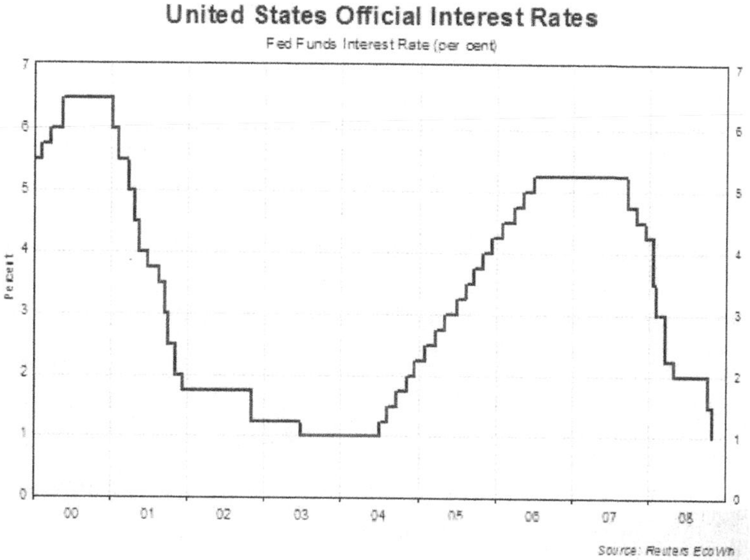

By 2003, there was no longer the need for any further deregulation or policy reform; lending institutions could essentially do whatever they desired to make a profit. Any mortgage product that could be imagined to get people to purchase homes was allowed. Interest rates were at historic lows and housing prices at historic highs. Above all, there was no risk to the originators of loans because they were simply selling their loans off immediately to 3rd party investors in the form of MBS. Mortgage application standards immediately dwindled. Almost anybody who asked for a loan got one and financiers just kept on bundling and selling those loans with no regard for their quality as an asset.

Loans were structured so that people could afford them initially but then would have no chance should they not be able to refinance later or if the property took even a slight decline in value. Teaser rate, interest only, balloon ARM, and several other 'Option ARM' loans became prevalent in the industry. Sometimes people were even given mortgages that put the homes underwater (negative equity) up to 25% right from the start, the logic being that with current appreciation rates they'd be fine in just two years. Further, people were given mortgages with very little to nothing down, indicating they were clearly overextending their finances beyond what they could afford. In 2005, the median down payment was two percent with over forty percent not making a down payment at all.[14] Nobody seemed to care that these people were set up to fail later (not even them), nor was the possibility that the market might level off or decrease at some point considered. These actions are perfect examples of 'predatory lending' which has been a focal point of public outrage and numerous lawsuits in recent years.

The savvy investors on Wall Street began to realize that this boom couldn't possibly be sustained and started betting against it with the use of credit default swaps (CDS). Essentially, a credit default swap acts similar to insurance against bond or security defaults. If an investor purchases a CDS against a mortgage backed security and then it goes bad, that investor gets paid. As the bubble grew exponentially, so did the use of CDS. Shrewd traders realized that at some point soon it must inevitably crash and at that point their investments would pay off enormously. The beauty of CDS for investors is that they are highly leveraged. A $10 million MBS could be "insured" by investments of less than $100,000.[15] These swaps became incredibly popular as the boom was reaching its peak and government agencies no longer regulated CDS (or any derivatives). Credit default swaps are genius if you are trading securities, though how one could not see issues would develop from their use is beyond me.

Investment banks took a similar initiative via off the books banking transactions collectively known as the shadow banking system. Shadow banking began to grow at the turn of the century and peaked in 2006 before crashing in 2007. At its peak, shadow banking assets represented nearly half of the total value of the banking industry as a whole.[14] The core of this system revolved around exotic financial instruments that allowed banks to get around regulation. These special investment vehicles allowed financial institutions to act privately and without oversight from anyone as they are technically accounted for as separate entities and therefore do not show up on the banks' balance sheets.

The foundation of these assets were MBS, so when traders realized these investments were not the low-risk ventures they were believed to be, they promptly stopped purchasing them. The immediate effect was their value declining sharply and investment banks literally started to go bankrupt overnight due to such rapid meltdowns in net worth. This is exactly what happened to Bear Stearns in 2008; its stock went from about eighty dollars a share down to two dollars per share in a 48 hour period.[16] As was the case with nearly all aspects of the housing bubble, this would never have become a problem had housing prices continuously risen but obviously that is impossible. Though the shadow banking system has largely collapsed in recent years, the effects linger on unfortunately. Many mortgages were bundled together, sliced, and diced with complete disregard for maintaining any semblance of a real asset and so today its often very difficult, if not impossible, to know who owns each individual mortgage note at all.

- Mortgage fraud reports increased 1,411% from 1997-2005.[14]
- Mortgage denial rates decreased from 29% to just 14% from 1998 to 2002.[14]
- From 1994-2006, subprime loans as a percentage of total mortgages went from 5% to over 20% while the amount of total loans simultaneously increased more than four-fold.[14]
- By end of 2006, the top five investment banks had about $4.1 trillion in debt with only minimal reserves (meaning a slight decrease in asset value = bankrupt). To put that in perspective, at the same time our nation's total debt was $8.5 trillion.[14]
- By the end of 2007, the outstanding CDS amount was $62.2 trillion.[17]

While the actions taken by the government, Federal Reserve, Wall Street, and major banking institutions over the last century certainly poised the nation for an imploding housing market, they cannot be blamed entirely. We must simultaneously take a look at the other side of the coin, namely the American public. It's a little tougher to swallow that our belief systems and our subsequent actions carry some of the blame also. Yes – our countrymen, you, and I are all guilty in some fashion. One glaring weakness to the common argument that the whole problem was set up by the financial institutions is that it fails to recognize the obvious counterpoint of "people still had to act for anything to happen". The government and Fed may have put lenders in a favorable position and given them too much power. The financial institutions may have abused that power and created traps for the common man. However at the end of the day, we have the final decision as to whether that loan for a home that is worth vastly beyond what we can afford is best for us. We as a people must accept this reality in order to grow.

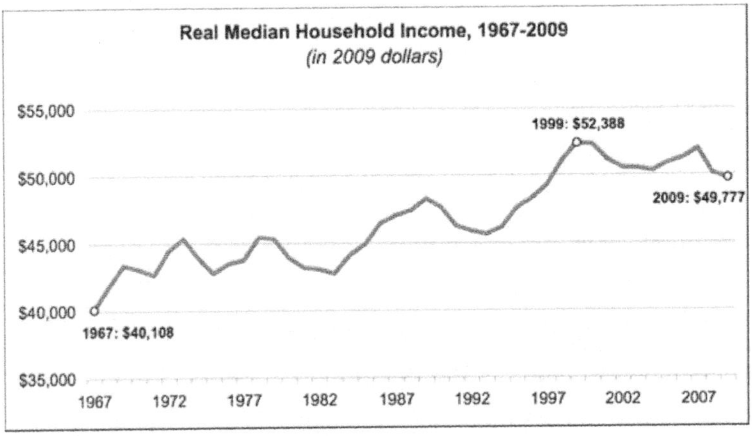

Many will argue that "we were duped". And there are merits to that argument. But, it is equally truthful that many people took as much advantage of the laws and policies as any institution did to live beyond their means. Our society as a whole buys into an entitlement complex whereby we believe that each of us deserves nothing but the highest standard of living, regardless of our means. The average median income (after adjusting for inflation) for individuals has remained nearly stagnant for over 50 years.[18] Moreover, inflation has caused the cost of living to rise consistently. Yet, almost all of us believe that we are entitled to more – better homes, cars, vacations, clothing, etc. I do not deny my own desires for greater things in my life, nor do I wish for others to settle for less. However, it is obviously irresponsible to live beyond our means consistently and by example teach the youth of our nation to do the same.

People constantly complain that "the middle class is dying". I'm sure you hear it as much as I do. While I understand where that viewpoint comes from, the reality is that income levels haven't changed much – it's our perception of middle class that has. Middle class was not always defined as two new cars in the driveway, a 2,000+ square foot home, nice dinners out every week, and a few vacations per year. If you look around, many chase exactly that believing that their social status depends upon it... and end up in enormous debt for the attempt. Living beyond our means has become a rather alarming epidemic in recent years. The average debt to income ratio for Americans went from 77% of income in 1990 all the way up to 127% in 2007 and is continuing an upward trend.[14] It doesn't take a mathematician to realize that long-term financial health cannot be maintained with debt that exceeds income, but that is the norm in this country today.

The vast majority of debt load for the average person is their home mortgage. The fact that debt ratios have risen so much indicates that people are overleveraging themselves to acquire property that is beyond their income level. Assuming that people are using logical reasoning for their purchase decisions, this brings forth the conclusion that most people believe that their home is a wise investment. There are a few reasons why people make this assumption but the fact remains that it is an inaccurate belief system.

Most people believe in the concept that home prices will consistently rise forever. While historically this is accurate over the long term, most people don't live in their homes for that long these days. In the few year period that they are living there the home may appreciate or depreciate, and it's difficult to assess which is more likely. Even when the home is rising in value, it is still not a great idea to view a primary residence as an investment. Regardless of gaining or losing value, residences produce negative cash flow on a monthly basis. Costs (mortgage interest, insurance, taxes, maintenance, etc.) vastly outweigh any capital gains in most cases and therefore nullify the investment aspect of the home. Housing costs are a necessary aspect of life and therefore purchasing a home is not necessarily a bad choice (though these days renting is looking like a better option frequently). It's the concept of perceiving your residence as being an investment and relying on its appreciation that is faulty.

People also tend to believe that their home saves them money as a tax shelter so they must buy a bigger, better house so they can write off the interest on their payments. Some of the less astute (or scrupulous) real estate agents and even some financial advisors advocate such a tactic, so I can see where people get the concept from. That doesn't make it any less ludicrous. If buying something beyond your means to write off the interest makes sense to you then I have the best program on earth to offer you! You can send me as much money as you'd like and for every dollar I receive I'll send you a quarter back. Of course I'm being facetious but perhaps now when you consider tax shelters, you'll be more discerning as to who the advice is coming from and seek alternative sources when things don't make sense. We all need to take an objective step back and assume a little responsibility for our [misguided] beliefs and actions.

The bottom line of the housing bubble is actually quite simple: housing prices continuously rose to the point of inevitable collapse and everyone (banks, investors, and citizens) over-leveraged themselves to take advantage of the boom. One could make a strong argument that the boom was caused by irresponsible actions taken by financial institutions and consumers out of greed. Nobody was forced to create loan products designed to fail and nobody was forced to accept those mortgages either.

Conversely, one could contest that the actions taken by the government and the Fed prompted logical responses from the people, investors, and bankers. Their actions over the last century ensured the continuous rise of home prices for many years. In fact, housing prices never came down over a ten year period from 1947-2007 (even after factoring in inflation).[19] Therefore, it seemingly made sense to risk all by purchasing homes and mortgage backed securities. To put it in perspective, if you went to the corner store and the same lotto numbers had hit almost every week for 60 weeks, you probably wouldn't consider it too risky to buy a whole bunch of lottery tickets with those numbers. While both sides make strong points, and it is an interesting debate, placing blame does us no good. The reality is that all parties were intimately involved and all made their share of judgment errors.

Part 2: Foreclosure 101

With 2006 nearing its end, the housing market leveled off briefly... then plummeted. The result of this prompt and surprising market turn was economic chaos. Loan originations reduced dramatically and home sales diminished. Many investment banks failed, received bailouts to survive, or were forced into mergers. Countless investors and corporate stockholders lost billions. Housing prices dropped at record rates over a short period of time. This left a massive quantity of homes in a negative equity state. Many of those crafty loans discussed previously now started to mature and people found themselves looking at payments that were unaffordable. These economic implications permeated all aspects of the U.S. economy. The foreclosure crisis stemmed from one repetitive sequence: people couldn't (or wouldn't) afford their homes anymore and couldn't sell the homes because they had no equity. Thus, many homeowners faced inevitable foreclosure proceedings.

All vested parties once again struggled to adapt to such rapid changes in the housing market. Policies were altered or created prematurely. Interest rates were tampered with unnecessarily. Numerous assets were liquidated or traded. And homeowners frantically searched for relief – most didn't find any. Once again, nobody had any regard for the long-term effects of their actions; they simply acted to escape financial destruction.

We will explore some details of this market crash and its effects, but I think it's critical to touch on something briefly first. Markets have always expanded and contracted, that is their nature. Bull and bear markets are not inherently good or bad, they simply represent the natural growth and retractions of an economy. Product costs, wages, and service fees are all examples of prices – and yes, all must go up and down at times. In the past, people didn't rely so much on market trends as they were much slower and more deliberate. Massive and rapid spikes upward or downward were unheard of. When markets are stable there is less panic and therefore fewer irrational actions are taken.

Our economy has grown much more volatile in recent years. This is due to the market being artificially adjusted frequently and accelerated communication. One small occurrence and within hours the whole nation knows about it and overreacts to it. Soon you see the entire market system alter within the course of a day or two, all because of one incident that could have been entirely inconsequential. It's difficult to place blame for that. We have grown overly cautious and sporadic in our decision-making as a natural reaction to the constant disruption of capitalism. Between overregulation in some industries, lack of regulation in others, interest rates constantly in flux, the media's mixed messages, and countless impingements upon the free market, it makes perfect sense not to trust in it.

It is my belief that the foreclosure crisis is a lot like many other economic issues of today – merely the result of overreactions and poor control. Don't take what I'm saying out of context. There have been many policies altered, laws implemented, and actions taken to effect the U.S. economy that are irreparable or close to it. But those actions can't or won't be undone anytime soon so we as citizens must focus on what remains within our sphere of influence and then push similar restraints onto those representing us in government.

The federal government adds, removes, or alters policies with little regard. Similarly, the Fed often adjusts rates too quickly and dramatically. These entities act without oversight and attempt to constantly control capitalism which is intended to be left alone for the most part. Oftentimes these changes make things worse than they were originally. The financial industry responds in kind and exploits each alteration to the maximum (i.e. deregulation means we must quadruple our loan output in just two years!). And the public simply closes their eyes and rides the wave with no regard for the long-term consequences (i.e. if they'll give me a 200k loan on a 25k per year income, I have to take it!).

Until we as a nation establish some systematic constraints and the majority of citizens exercise self-control, the market will continue on the path of instability. We will see more booms and busts, consistently experiencing an irrational marketplace. Left unhampered, the economy would quickly become more supportive to society. Awareness of this concept is crucial so that we may work as individuals and as one people to improve.

Absolute turmoil in the market occurred between 2006 and 2010. The bulk of the damage came between June of 2006 and September of 2008 when housing prices declined by an unprecedented 20%.[14] This price decrease was accompanied by drastic increases in personal credit balances and unemployment rates. Many of those who remained employed found themselves facing lower wages or reduced hours. Lower or non-existent incomes combined with higher debt loads and worsening loan terms pushed families to the edge financially.

Many decided to voluntarily enter foreclosure rather than face the financial implications of keeping their home. *Yes, for about 18% of homeowners during this time period it made financial sense to lose their home.*[20] Ironically, the majority of those who decided to "strategically foreclose" were those with the highest credit ratings to begin with. For them it was simply a mathematical equation: Does it cost more to have poor credit for a few years or to pay 50-200% more for a home than it's worth? For many the answer was the latter and so they walked away. Others were more stubbornly attached to their homes for sentimental reasons. Most homeowners facing this prospect simply didn't have the means to move on even if they wanted to. These people were in an untenable position, forced to idly observe as their finances toppled.

The steps leading to foreclosure are very similar throughout the United States. After being late on a mortgage payment by fifteen days or thereabouts, the lender sends out a notice demanding payment. Two or more reminder letters are generally sent to the borrower over the following weeks. Ninety days after payments have ceased, the loan is officially in default. Another letter advising the homeowner of the defaulted loan is mailed. Borrowers will often begin to receive calls from their bank during this time to advise them of what is taking place and what they may do about it.

At this stage, homeowners have the right to reinstate their loan which means paying for all missed payments plus any interest and penalties that have accrued. The time frame allowed to reinstate by right varies in each state but regardless, doing so cures the default and prevents the foreclosure process from starting. Should homeowners be unable or unwilling to reinstate their loan, the foreclosure process can start at any time. Upon reaching that point, reinstatement may or may not remain an option.

Foreclosure means that secured real property is being seized and sold by the lender to recoup its investment upon the borrower's failure to keep the loan current. The foreclosure process is much less clear as it varies widely in each state. This is a big reason why it's so difficult for people to find sound advice as to what to expect and how to protect themselves – what's effective in one state might not be in another or may not even exist.

There are two basic types of foreclosures: judicial and non-judicial. Judicial foreclosure means that you are notified by receiving a complaint from your local circuit court. Ownership of the note must be proved in accord of law and a judgment must be issued to pursue seizure of the property. Non-Judicial foreclosure notification consists of an advertisement of some sort, usually in the form of a letter, a notice posted on the property or a public forum, and/or a notice published in a local newspaper. There is generally a process whereby you can work with the lender to retain the property. If this is not successful, the home goes to auction.

Twenty-two states primarily utilize the judicial process while twenty-eight states generally rely on foreclosure by advertisement. Some of them allow the use of both procedures depending upon certain conditions. While most states in each category follow similar processes, each has its own intricacies that homeowners in that state must be aware of – the primary variance being timelines. Appendix A outlines how each state generally handles foreclosures. Make sure to utilize that tool as you're reading so that you may better understand how the information provided applies to your residence's location.

While notification and legal procedures vary, the end result is almost always the same: the property is auctioned to the highest bidder. Trustees, Sheriffs, or Courts process these auctions, depending on which state the property is located in. Opening bid amounts are determined by the lender and generally equate to the remaining balance of the loan plus interest, penalties, and any fees. Sometimes the bidding starts at a reduced amount for varying reasons. Regardless of the opening bid, the property is sold to the highest bidder which can be a private investor but is most often the lender itself. This is because most homes going to foreclosure are upside down and therefore private investors avoid them.

If the auction is won by an individual, it must be paid for in full within 24 hours. Should the lender take the property back, it can submit a credit bid as it is retaining its own asset. Whoever wins the auction gets the property with clear title, aside from property taxes – any junior liens are extinguished. If the auction is won by the lender, the home becomes a Real Estate Owned (REO) property. The bank can then do with it what they please – usually list it for sale, and usually for much less than the foreclosure sale amount.

In some states, there is a period of time in the latter part of the foreclosure process known as the redemption period. This period can be after a judgment is issued by the court and before the auction is held. Alternatively, it can be after the auction sale is conducted – it depends on the state. The redemption period is a predetermined time frame during which the borrower may retain their property by paying the full amount of the judgment or auction price, plus interest. The amount of time to redeem varies widely from not existing in some states to a full year in others (two years in Tennessee). Redemption can be a powerful tool for homeowners seeking to relieve themselves of foreclosure as it essentially nullifies all of the previous proceedings. Borrowers can pay the amount themselves to keep their property or they can sell the home to a third party. If the latter, the sale must close during the redemption period and for as much or more than is owed. This right is especially useful to homeowners in those rare circumstances whereby the amount necessary to redeem is less than the value of the property.

Once this period passes, or if there is no right of redemption, eviction proceedings are the final step. Most states require that the new owner of the property file a separate action in court or provide specific notice of a date occupants must relocate by. Should the occupants remain in the home once a court order is obtained or that time period notified expires, a Sheriff can remove the occupants from the home physically.

With the general foundation of how foreclosures are conducted laid, delving into the particulars of each type of foreclosure is warranted. As stated previously, the start of a judicial foreclosure proceeding begins with the service of a complaint from the lender upon the homeowner. Upon receipt, homeowners then have a period of time (usually 20-30 days) during which they can respond to that complaint and raise any issues to contest the foreclosure that they may have. It is highly recommended to all homeowners at this stage that they file an answer with the court. Without an answer they face a default judgment, meaning the lender gets the judgment of foreclosure automatically. Any defense, even a weak one, will at least delay the process and give the homeowner time to make arrangements. A strong defense can drastically delay the process or prevent the foreclosure entirely. Once an answer to the complaint has been filed, the case proceeds like any other civil matter – motions may be filed, discovery can be obtained, a jury may be requested (demanded in some states), and ultimately a judge rules one way or the other.

Assuming a judgment is obtained by the lender, the next step is a Publication of Sale. This is a publicized notice that the property will be auctioned off at a specified date, time, and place. Most states have statutory time frames for publication that must be met prior to the sale. Foreclosure auctions are conducted with the title to the home going to the highest bidder free and clear (except for any property tax liens). If there is a redemption period allowed, that time period must pass prior to the auction winner taking possession of the property (unless the home is deemed abandoned). Title automatically conveys to the new owner upon closing of the redemption period if no repurchase or sale of the property is completed.

The final step of the foreclosure process is eviction. In most states, the titleholder of the property will file a District Court Landlord-Tenant complaint to evict, with the hearing usually set seven to fourteen days from the date of filing. At that hearing a Writ of Eviction will usually be granted and the occupants are court ordered to leave within a judge-determined time period (generally 1-30 days). Should the occupants not leave within that time period voluntarily, a Sheriff will remove them and their property from the home. At this point, the foreclosure process is officially complete and all of the original homeowner's interests, legal and possessory, are extinguished entirely.

People residing in non-judicial foreclosure states are not so fortunate with regards to the process utilized. The notice time is significantly reduced and there is no automatic court involvement. While lenders attempting to foreclose in judicial states may have incentive to work amicably with homeowners (i.e. to avoid extensive litigation costs), those in non-judicial states do not have that same enticement. In non-judicial states the bank essentially acts as judge, jury, and executioner if left unchecked – it is up to the homeowner to contest foreclosure if they so choose. Otherwise, the foreclosing party need not prove ownership of the note attached to the home, that all foreclosure requirements were met, or anything else for that matter.

Non-judicial foreclosures are simple and fast-paced, averaging less than half the time of a judicial foreclosure. After the Letter of Default has been received, homeowners should be prepared for the foreclosure process to begin fairly quickly. Generally about 30 days later, a Notice of Sale will be published in the local legal news and then served upon the homeowner. This notice indicates when and where the auction of the home will take place. Auctions can be held in any public forum, though usually they will take place at the local court house – the timeframe varies widely by state.

Some states have implemented a mandatory offering of mediation from lender to borrower to formally attempt to resolve the matter amicably. If your state has this requirement, it would be during this time period that mediation requests would be received. It is always in the best interest of the homeowner to respond to these requests and attend mediation as it can only help and at the very least delays the process. Homeowners in non-judicial states must take advantage of any opportunities to protect themselves because they are few. On the scheduled date and time, the auction is held publically with the highest bidder obtaining the ownership rights to the property. The majority of non-judicial states then allow for a redemption period to give the homeowner one final opportunity to retain their property.

Upon the passing of this time period, an eviction proceeding will commence to obtain a Writ of Eviction and force removal of all occupants from the property in 1-30 days. In states which have no redemption period, this eviction process will take place soon after the auction is held. Generally, homeowners have the right to contest an eviction complaint if they so choose – without filing as Plaintiff, this is the borrower's only time to have an argument heard by a judge in non-judicial states. Should no defense come forth, the Writ will likely be issued and then the occupants can voluntarily leave the property within the ordered time frame or a Sheriff will remove them upon its expiration. As with judicial foreclosure, it is at this time that all legal and possessory interests in the home are no longer applicable and the foreclosure is complete.

If the foreclosure process is so simple, why is there always such controversy over it? The answer is "Securitization". Foreclosure is an incredibly simple procedure with little to no debate if the original lender forecloses on the original borrower. However, that is rarely the case. If you recall in Part 1, most loans were immediately sold off to investors once they were originated. This transforms the loan originator from lender to servicer, meaning that they merely handle (service) the loan on behalf of the investor. From there, loans can be transferred again, bundled together, and converted into other assets. Servicers can change periodically as well at the discretion of the investor.

Securitization of mortgages is a complex topic but the basis of it is easy enough to grasp. A borrower takes out a loan from an originator. The originator takes multiple loans and groups them together, usually within a special investment vehicle (SIV). The most common SIV is known as a real estate mortgage investment conduit (REMIC). SIVs are held within trusts, which are governed by Pooling and Servicing agreements. The Pooling and Servicing agreements indicate exactly how those trusts are to handle their assets.

The most common scenario, though not the only one, is for the loans held in the REMIC to be converted into stock and sold on the open market. Those stocks can then be traded like any other paper asset and so they are passed around amongst varying entities. The problem with this is that stocks cannot be legally re-converted back into loans. Even if they could be, it would be impossible to know who owns any given loan because every shareholder would have a piece of every loan in that REMIC.

This issue of determining ownership of a particular loan is where the majority of the controversy arises from. This topic is further complicated by the sheer complexity of these SIVs and the trusts which control them. A typical Pooling and Servicing agreement is at least 300 pages of small print containing specific courses of action for each of many different scenarios that may occur with its assets and also assigns each asset into specific tranches for simplification.

An additional dispute stems from this approach to loan securitization – recording requirements. It is perfectly legal for a loan to be transferred from one entity to another, assuming the transfer is properly performed. Traditionally, a proper transfer must include reasonable compensation for the asset and for the assignment (transfer) to be recorded with the local Register of Deeds. Obviously, the above scenario does not meet those requirements. So how do banks get around that? They wondered the same thing, and thus worked together to manifest MERS.

The MERS system is a subject of much scrutiny. Many cases have been tried regarding the validity of the system and numerous books and articles discussing the topic have been released over the past few years. Mortgage

Electronic Registration System, Inc. (MERS) is a privately held company whose members include thousands of lenders, servicers, investors, and government institutions that was forged by and for the mortgage banking industry. MERS created and maintains a database that tracks mortgages for its members as they are transferred from bank to bank. By tracking loan transfers electronically, MERS has largely eliminated the practice of lenders recording an assignment of a mortgage with the appropriate county every time the loan is sold. The chaos that has ensued since its inception is well documented. It doesn't take a genius to figure out that if all major lenders can freely transfer mortgages between themselves without oversight, there will eventually be problems with proving ownership. MERS does not lend money or service loans, yet often acts as Mortgagee and files suit as a foreclosing party. Most of the lawsuits regarding foreclosures from the wrong party stem from this system's failure to properly transfer mortgages. Some states have ruled against MERS' operations and others have upheld that what MERS does is legal, though I'm still not quite sure how the judges in those states could have viewed its actions as just.

So originators bundled loans and placed them into SIVs, trusts holding the SIVs dictated that the assets be sold, and all transfers are harbored in the MERS system to avoid any necessity for traditional assignment recordation. As shady as that is, it gets worse. The robosigning scandal was unveiled in 2010 and for a short period surrounding that humiliation, banks halted the majority of foreclosure proceedings. Robosigning refers to the practice of unqualified mortgage industry employees signing documents that they haven't read or affixing signatures of other qualified employees to documents without consent. This practice occurred at incredible rates, with counties often seeing hundreds of the same person's signature on mortgage documents, in dozens of different writing styles. At the time, this was unheard of; today there are lists of hundreds of known robosigners for public use (See Appendix C). Despite numerous promises to eliminate such practices, robosigning still occurs today. Obviously, any document that can be proven to be executed in this fashion should be considered void.

How can you tell if your mortgage was securitized?
There is a reference to an investor or a trust in your mortgage or foreclosure documentation.
Your documentation indicates a message to the effect of "We are a debt collector trying to collect a debt".
Your loan was originated by a local bank or one that is now out of business and is now held by a major lender.
If you are a bit more sophisticated in your approach, you can search for it on the SEC website (www.sec.gov).

Between blatant evidence of fraudulent practices, publicly traded entities holding bifurcated assets, and an openly utilized shield to protect it all from public view (MERS), one would think that almost any foreclosure would be immediately thwarted by pointing out that it's likely to be unlawful. That is not the case though. There are two primary reasons for this. The first is that all of this information has been overly simplified and in reality is much more difficult to decipher [Remember, accusations must be proven]. Suffice to say that this complexity bars the majority of people from ever fully understanding what happened to their loan. They are not alone – most attorneys and judges don't get it either. They cannot rule something unlawful if they don't comprehend it. Further, there is a common mentality that "You took out a loan so you must pay for it regardless". Though not entirely accurate, there is some validity to that argument and that's a big reason that foreclosure defense has a negative stigma attached to it.

It is evident that the foreclosure process is skewed in the lender's favor in most states, regardless of whether that state operates in a judicial or non-judicial manner. This makes sense as foreclosure is justified as long as the proper actions are taken prior to commencement. Mortgages are secured debts and the security collateral of the loan is the property it is attached to – no payment of the debt means the property goes to the lender. That said, there are significant defects in how foreclosures are handled in many cases which warrant defensive tactics by borrowers, especially in non-judicial states. Regrettably, there are no preventative measures in place to ensure that these errors and inadequacies are corrected. Homeowners are responsible for protecting themselves if they want any security from unjust foreclosures. Fortunately, sufficient defenses are available in many instances – they simply have to be implemented properly and in a timely fashion.

Part 3: Stand up for yourself!

Understanding the history and procedures behind foreclosure is important, but what do you do about it once you know? It depends. Most people search for 'the answer' but it simply doesn't exist without ones individual goals, circumstances, and finances factored in. Based on those criterion, different possibilities may or may not be available to you. Some available opportunities include keeping your home, removing debt loads, repairing credit, or benefitting financially from your property. An additional option that can be highly beneficial but is often overlooked is temporarily retaining the property to save money and relocate gracefully. The most important thing is to be decisive, regardless of which choice you make. The more time that passes, the less options you will have and the less effective they will likely be.

The most common objective sought by homeowners is retaining their property. This is also the most difficult end result to obtain for most because doing so primarily revolves around satisfactory finances, something that is often lacking for people in this position. The first aspect to consider is your property's equity state – if the home is significantly underwater, it likely doesn't make sense to even try to keep it. The only time this decision may be altered is after the auction of the property, under very specific circumstances. The property must sell at a lower price than the loan amount, must be in a state with a right of redemption, and you must have access to funds to redeem the home – not a common scenario.

Essentially, if the home isn't in a balanced or positive equity state, it is best to focus on other alternatives. Otherwise, you are setting yourself up to fail sooner or later. It should be noted that there is one exception to this rule – principal reduction loan modifications. These do exist and are possible to obtain with proper qualifications and leverage, but are quite rare (<5% of homeowners in foreclosure get one).[21] If a borrower is willing to pursue a principal reduced loan modification whole-heartedly, and is comfortable with the risk (i.e. can make other arrangements if it fails), it may be possible to manually adjust the equity position of the home. However, it would be irresponsible to recommend this tactic to the majority of homeowners.

Assuming the property has equity, the next factor to think about is your personal finances. As a general rule, household income should exceed mortgage payments by at least threefold and savings should total at least three months' income. Should your household meet these minimum recommendations, retaining the property is likely possible and fiscally responsible. If not, you must seriously question whether it is wise to invest beyond your means in this particular property. The honest answer is usually "no" but that response does not readily come to mind when talking about your home. A person's home is their sanctuary; a place of peace where their family can reside in security and comfort – giving that up is not a concept most people are willing to entertain.

If your household does not meet the income and savings guidelines above, that does not mean it is impossible to keep your home. It does mean that should you be successful in retaining the house, you will be at significantly greater risk for future financial difficulty. Disposable income will be minimal or non-existent due to a disproportionate amount of income being directed to your living expenses. I'm not trying to discourage you from working to keep your home, but these risks are real and should not be taken lightly. If you are facing foreclosure and wish to remain in your home permanently you should make absolute certain that you understand and are comfortable with all associated risk factors and necessary sacrifices that will come with being in a financially overextended state. You should also take a step back and look at where you are currently in the foreclosure process. If you haven't gotten into to default yet or have just recently been notified of default, your chances of keeping the home are good. Beyond that point, your odds of retaining your property dwindle significantly.

OK, so you've determined that it is possible and financially wise to work to retain your home – now what? Once again, it depends. Traditional methods of retaining property include reinstating the loan, modifying the loan, and redeeming the property from foreclosure, depending on what stage the foreclosure process is at and the state the home is located in. Reinstatement is by far the easiest method of keeping any home – simply bring your payments up to date along with any interest and penalties. Reinstatement does not require any complex paperwork, legal maneuvering, or approval from the lender. In addition to keeping the home, reinstatement positively affects your credit which may have been tarnished by this time. This tactic is the best choice if you had a short term hardship and have since rectified the situation.

Should reinstatement not be possible (either due to lack of funds or being past that time frame in the foreclosure process), loan modification is the next step. Loan modifications can be great. They may lower monthly payments, interest rates, and even principal balances. Loans can be modified at any time from default to auction sale, or even after that in some cases. The biggest problem with loan modification is that it must be approved by the lender, and this is a much tougher feat than you might expect – less than ten percent of loan mods are approved.[22] It is impossible to determine in advance if you will qualify and be approved because no standard system for approval has been released to date. Further, each different lender and government-sponsored program has different qualification standards. The other problem with loan modifications is that even if approved, sometimes they don't help or can even make matters worse. Often the reformed loan offer doesn't have significantly better terms or the modification provides for temporary "help" with low payments and/or interest rates which then drastically increase after a certain time period or are accompanied by a massive balloon payment. Obviously that's not something anyone wants, but desperate people make desperate decisions at times and so these types of terms are frequently accepted. This can be fine in certain circumstances, but is generally not recommended and is something you should be mindful of.

Applying for a loan modification is easy enough; simply go to your lender's website and request it online or call and have a representative send you the forms. A list of phone and fax numbers for many common loan servicers has been provided in Appendix B. Once a loan modification has been applied for, instructions will come from your lender regarding additional documents that need to be filled out and supporting documents necessary for review. These generally include forms to release tax return information, pay stubs, W-2s, 1099s, utility bills, bank statements, and a hardship letter, as well as any forms that the individual lender specifies. Each document should always include the loan number so as to be properly identified and then faxed to the number indicated within the loan modification package. There is always a specified time frame to return the documentation which must be fully completed. Make sure the time limits that are given are strictly adhered to and every document is fully completed as denied loan modifications for incomplete paperwork or inadequate submission timing are common. Once everything is in and satisfactory, the review process will begin which can take anywhere from a couple of weeks to several months. Oftentimes numerous requests for additional or revised documentation will be made. Patience is key – this process can get extremely redundant and irritating.

Upon completion of the review process, you will receive written correspondence from the loan servicer indicating an approval, denial, or trial period for a potential loan mod. If approved, the terms should be carefully reviewed prior to entering into the agreement to ensure the terms are acceptable based on your specific financial picture. Assuming the terms are favorable, acceptance is as simple as signing a few documents and then resuming the dictated payment schedule. Many modification approvals come with a caveat – trial periods. This is a three month period during which a specified payment sum must be made to the lender in a timely fashion "in good faith" to then obtain a permanent modification. A permanent loan mod is not guaranteed but has a much higher probability of being granted should the trial payments be made timely. Denial is the most likely response unfortunately. Whether immediate or after a trial payment plan, denial of the loan modification usually means that foreclosure efforts will be escalated shortly and you should be prepared to seek alternative options.

The most common reaction to loan mod denial is "Why?" – a logical response, especially if you appear to qualify. There is not a one-size-fits-all answer but generally speaking, this is because your "lender" cannot modify your loan for you. Usually the "lender" you are dealing with is actually your loan servicer, even if you are dealing with the bank that you took the loan out with. This is due to the fact that most loans have been securitized and sold as explained in Part 2. Loan servicers do not own your note, they simply handle it for the actual lender (or more often an investor). Therefore they do not have the power to modify your loan. Only when a loan has defaulted can the originator buy it back. They don't have to buy it back, but if they do it comes at a steep discount because it's now a non-performing asset. Should that occur, your loan may be modified, but that rules out the majority of people.

If all efforts to reinstate or modify the loan have failed, the next step in working to retain your home is to evaluate your state's foreclosure laws (See Appendix A) and your ability to access funds. Is your state judicial or non-judicial? Does it allow for a redemption period? How does your state handle deficiencies? Assuming redemption is possible, do you have the means to utilize that option? These are the important questions that must be asked and answered before deciding on your next action plan. If your state allows for the right of redemption, and you have the means to capitalize on that right, such would be a sure-fire way to keep the property. Bide your time until the judgment of foreclosure has been granted (judicial) or the foreclosure sale has been completed (non-judicial), then request a redemption payoff from the foreclosing party. Pay that sum within the designated time period and the house is yours free and clear. An added bonus of redeeming the home is that it drastically repairs the credit rating of the homeowner. A word of caution about deficiencies: Most states allow them to be pursued. A deficiency judgment can be a real thorn in your side so be prepared for that possibility as well if your state allows for it and your redemption price was less than the total amount that was owed.

Redemption is not usually possible. Not every state allows for that right and even when available, the majority of homeowners do not have the means to capitalize on it. When in this position, the only remaining option to permanently retain property is through strategic litigation efforts. This less traditional avenue has its pros and cons just like every other relief effort. The benefits can be fantastic. In a situation where the foreclosure was wrongful, a well-presented and argued case can stop or overturn the foreclosure entirely. Many lenders are weary of pursuing foreclosure as adamantly once ample defenses have been raised. This may lead to a favorable settlement – generally a loan modification that wouldn't have been available otherwise. The downsides of litigating are significant as well though. There is no guarantee that litigation will prevent foreclosure proceedings or allow you to keep your home. Litigation is expensive, time consuming, and stressful. That expenditure can sometimes be justified though as house payments are not made during litigation.

I believe that some actions regarding foreclosure defense can be successfully undertaken without legal counsel. Other projects are best suited to having an attorney represent you though and you should be aware of that. Part of the reason for that is complexity; some legal arguments are very difficult to prepare. The other part is that judges and other attorneys like to deal with lawyers, not common people. It's an elitist mentality to be sure, but it's a reality none the less. Below is a chart outlining which courses of action you should be okay to pursue on your own and which you should seek assistance for. If you don't feel comfortable with some of the actions I state you should be able to handle alone and can afford assistance, don't be ashamed – get the help you need (you'll save a ton of headache). Conversely, if you understand the more complex issues but want representation or have more time than funds available, one option is to do your own research and rough drafts, then hire an attorney on an a la carte basis to format, revise, file, and represent you for one or more specific tasks.

This tactic can save a lot of money and ensure you are always aware of what arguments are being presented on your behalf.

Do it Yourself (Pro Per)	Seek Representation
Reinstatement/Loan modification/Redemption	Short Sale (real estate agent, not lawyer)
Contesting foreclosure in court for time	Contesting foreclosure in court to keep home
Negotiating settlements for junior mortgages	Suing for damages in court
Chapter 7 Bankruptcy	Chapter 13 Bankruptcy

Electing to travel the path of litigation to retain property is one that should not be taken lightly. If you're considering this option you should always keep in mind that the law and justice are not necessarily the same thing, meaning that you could have been wronged by your lender but that doesn't always mean that the judge will see it that way and rule in your favor. When contesting foreclosure, much depends on the state in which you reside, your legal counsel (or lack thereof), and the judge assigned to your case.

Even if all legal factors line up in your favor, personal finances still play a large role as well. Many attorneys do a great job arguing cases and many judges are equitable in their decisions, but if you can't afford the home, there is nothing they can do about that. If the foreclosure is overturned and the mortgage is reinstated, can you make the payments or will the foreclosure process simply be reinitiated shortly thereafter? Similarly, should litigation efforts procure a favorable loan modification as a settlement to dismiss the case, will you be able to maintain the payments? A negative or uncertain response to either of these questions indicates that litigation is unlikely to be a wise option for you to entertain. Proceeding with litigation remains a viable option if you can answer affirmatively to those questions.

> Do not buy into any garbage you hear about obtaining a "free house" by suing your lender. This has occurred in some extreme cases but is highly unlikely. The goal is to retain your home with reasonable loan terms, not exploit your bank via the judicial system.

Litigious efforts must be pursued unreservedly to have any chance of success. Foreclosure defense has a negative stigma attached to it and banks are very powerful, so an uphill battle must always be anticipated. You must be prepared to face significant hostility from opposing counsels and judges, expend ample time and money, and cope with the stress associated with unknown results. As stated previously, being right doesn't necessarily equate to winning. Emerging as the victor in the court room greatly depends upon who's involved, application of proper statutes, citation of appropriate case law, and timing – not just a worthy argument. For this reason, it is almost mandatory to have a competent attorney represent you if you seek permanent retention of your home. Competent is the key word there – many lawyers are available in any given area but only a select few specialize in foreclosure defense. When choosing counsel, be sure to obtain and contact several references; reviewing some of the attorney's pleadings is wise as well. What was effective a few years ago or in other states may not have any positive implications now or in your state. Case law is constantly evolving and due to foreclosure being a big topic these days, statutes and legal procedures relating to it are consistently updated as well. A good attorney will have a firm understanding of and keep up to date on these changes. Prior to interviews, be sure to check out Appendix A for laws in your state. The functional glossary in Appendix F is helpful too – you don't want to go into a consultation with a lawyer and get confused with jargon.

With a trustworthy attorney in your corner, the specifics of your case can be reviewed and discussed so as to apply the proper arguments, statutes, and citations. There are five common themes for arguments which can be effective depending on varying circumstances. These include unconscionability of the mortgage, improper foreclosure process, lack of standing, egregious mortgage servicer errors, and unfair lending practices. Other claims exist, but most have been consistently ruled against or are considered to be extremist. Some radical arguments have been effectively applied under specific conditions, but the vast majority of situations do not call for such claims. If your case warrants such an immoderate petition, your attorney may guide you in its application.

Unconscionability of the mortgage applies primarily to those who have mental disabilities or lack fluent English. This argument revolves around the concept of equity (fairness) and essentially states that the homeowner was pushed into an agreement whereby he or she was doomed to failure from the onset unknowingly.

A more commonly used claim is that of unfair lending practices, which usually cite the Fair Debt Collection Practices Act (FDCPA), Real Estate Settlement Procedures Act (RESPA) or the Truth In Lending Act (TILA). These are federal regulations that are designed to protect homeowners from unfair lending practices. Frankly, arguments of this nature are much more effective for junior mortgages or obtaining damages than retaining property and thus should be applied as secondary arguments for primary mortgages, if used at all. Egregious mortgage servicer errors are not as rare as you might think. The best example of this is seen when reinstatement quotas are unduly inflated which prevents the homeowner from keeping their home in the easiest fashion. If you could have afforded the amount owed, but couldn't come up with the artificially inflated sum, this argument can be effectively applied. RESPA arguments only apply to junior liens, not the loan which funded the purchase of the home, so that limits the power of that particular law considerably. However, if proven to be violated, it does have the power to rescind equity or refinance loans.

A quick insight into junior mortgages is warranted here. In some cases, full mortgage payments are unable to be made or the home is upside down not due to the primary mortgage, but rather one or more additional loans that are secured by the property. If such is the case for you, there is perhaps another route for keeping your home available – settling the junior lien(s) for a reduced sum. This is a much easier and more common practice than you might expect, and it often makes sense for both sides to reach an agreement. Should your first mortgage amount be equal to or greater than the value of your home, any other mortgages are essentially unsecured debts as if you failed to make your payments and foreclosure occurred, those additional lienholders would not receive any funds. That gives you a powerful bargaining chip. Sometimes all it takes to get back on track is to get on the phone and negotiate a deal with the lender(s) that hold those additional mortgage loans.

Example: Your house is worth $200,000 and you can only afford to make a $2,000 per month mortgage payment. Your first mortgage is for $200,000 with a $2,000 per month payment amount, but you also have a HELOC loan for $50,000 with a $500 per month payment. You have some money saved up but you don't want to tap into that in case you end up losing your home and might need it then. You get on the phone and work out a deal with your HELOC lender. They agree to cancel the loan in exchange for $10,000 (20% of the loan – not uncommon at all) due to the fact that you are otherwise facing foreclosure and they'll be entitled to exactly zero. You pay them off and resume your now comfortable $2,000 per month payments, thus avoiding foreclosure. Everybody wins.

Lack of proper standing is one of the two most common and effective arguments against foreclosure. You are stating plainly that the foreclosing party does not own the note which is attached to the property they are trying to seize and therefore they can't foreclose. If a break in the chain of title can be proven adequately, this argument can have great success in overturning or preventing a foreclosure action.

An equally popular and successful claim is that of the lender's failure to adhere to state requirements relative to foreclosure. Should the foreclosing party insufficiently observe the foreclosure process, and this can be proven adequately, generally the judge will order the foreclosure to be restarted. Please note that the lack of adherence must be significant – arguing that your notice was improper due to your name being misspelled, for example, will likely be dismissed summarily in short order. These arguments are often available if thorough research is performed when compiling your complaint due to the common securitization practices illustrated in Part 2.

Understanding the assertions that your attorney intends to make on your behalf is critical. Homeowners must be comfortable with the associated costs, timelines, and risks for their cases or it doesn't make sense to proceed. As with most things, risk tends to coincide with reward, meaning that more conservative arguments will generally lead to more conservative outcomes while more aggressive claims can yield more beneficial results, but have a higher likelihood of failure as well. Deciding on how to pursue your rights in court is a very personal decision as each individual has varying comfort levels pertaining to litigation.

After choosing an attorney, discussing your options, and electing which claims you intend to pursue, it's best to allow your trusted counsel to operate as he or she sees fit with only cursory oversight. Your due diligence has been performed at this point and now is the time for your lawyer to apply your arguments properly using the correct statutes, case law citations, and proof requirements. All three of those differ drastically between states so leaving this to the professionals is almost necessary and certainly advised; trying to apply case law that held up in New York while contesting foreclosure in California is not likely to be successful for example. While you don't want to impose upon your attorney, it is always a good idea to request copies of each document filed on your behalf for your own records.

While no two states have exactly the same foreclosure processes, related statutes, or case law, there are some general themes seen nationally. It is easier to raise defenses in judicial states as compared to non-judicial states due to the requirements of proving the foreclosure to be proper in court. In non-judicial states, arguments usually must be raised by the homeowner as Plaintiff. Federal courts tend to be more favorable to homeowners than state courts. Cases heard in federal courts have more uniform procedures and allow for a greater variety of applicable case law. Honestly, the judges are often more qualified and educated on this aspect of law as well. Some claims are not well-received or understood by judges that are unfamiliar with foreclosure arguments, which is more common in state courts.

Homeowners represented by well-respected counsel often fare better than those battling in Pro Per (no attorney), even when raising identical claims, as judges and other attorneys tend to prefer to deal with lawyers. The firms used by lenders to process foreclosures are very repetitive – collectively known as foreclosure mills. This can be used to your advantage if your attorney has experience with these types of suits because he or she will likely know the tendencies of that mill. A list of the major foreclosure mills in each state can be seen in Appendix D. There are of course other tendencies that pervade all or most states. The bottom line is that it is almost always best to focus on retaining the most competent attorney available and allow that person to guide you without significant interference to take advantage of these trends – a good lawyer will know them in and out.

As odd as it may seem, bankruptcy court is actually the friendliest forum for homeowners to contest foreclosure. This is because bankruptcy trustees will require creditors to prove they have an interest in an asset in order to try to collect on it and that is difficult, if not impossible, to do if the loan has been securitized. Contesting foreclosure in bankruptcy court is called an adversary proceeding and is only available via Chapter 13 Bankruptcy. If your attorney thinks your case would bode well in this court, this is a viable option. Bankruptcy will be discussed more thoroughly later in this chapter.

Once you have filed your complaint (non-judicial) or answer and counter-complaint (judicial), you will want to immediately file a Lis Pendens with the local Register of Deeds. A Lis Pendens makes a public property title record that there is pending litigation and prevents a transfer of clear title to another party. This means that if your home is auctioned off and you win your case, the sale can be undone. This also means that no title insurance company will insure title to the purchaser of the home. You should also send Discovery requests right away. Oftentimes, bank errors cannot be proven without internal documents which can only be garnered in this fashion. From there, case progression depends on actions taken by other parties and the advice of your attorney based on specific case circumstances.

There are pros and cons to each type of foreclosure state at this juncture that you should be aware of. In non-judicial states, you may face escrow payments while you are contesting foreclosure. Escrow payments are monthly sums you pay to the court to ensure the lender is protected while you argue against it. It's ridiculous when there are legitimate issues of fact, and is not always ordered, but if it is and you fail to pay it you will lose your home to eviction even if your case is still active (though if you filed a Lis Pendens and win you could get it back). On the plus side, if you are ruled against, you can appeal the decision to a higher court which is a valuable asset as many lower courts are unfavorable to homeowners. In judicial states, you won't have to worry about an escrow order in most cases. But, you will need to make sure your case is well-presented from the start because you will not usually have the opportunity to appeal.

There are three possible outcomes to your litigious efforts to keep your home. The first is that you can be ruled against. In judicial states, this means you can contest no further and your home will be auctioned off very soon. You should prepare to move and not wait for an eviction order because that will make it difficult to rent a new home. In non-judicial states, you can appeal (maybe more than once), but if you ultimately lose, the same advice applies. The second possibility is that the judge rules in your favor. Depending on your argument and your state, this can mean anything from a foreclosure proceeding being forced to restart and be performed properly to obtaining damages to you getting clear title to your home and everything in between. The final option is a settlement between you and the foreclosing party. Again, this can mean a variety of different things – ranging from cash for keys (specified time to vacate with a certain monetary sum provided upon relocation) to a loan modification to you getting the house free and clear and everything in between. Consult with your attorney regarding settlement negotiations to ensure you get one that benefits you most should any offers become available.

If you agree to a settlement, be weary of the type of dismissal that is submitted. For an agreement whereby you are relinquishing the property, dismissal with prejudice (can't raise issues again) is warranted. This is also proper if you are getting the property free and clear or are obtaining compensation in lieu of same. Make sure the case is dismissed without prejudice if your settlement is looser, such as allowing you to modify your loan or restarting the foreclosure process by rescinding the previous foreclosure. You want to be protected if for some reason it doesn't work out.

Retaining property permanently may not be wise, possible, or comfortable for some people. That's a hard reality to face for some homeowners but once accepted, it opens up some other options. Being honest with yourself is critical – if keeping the home is highly unlikely or simply doesn't make sense financially, then why apply time, money, and effort to that cause? This does not mean giving up and succumbing to the foreclosure but rather utilizing other opportunities to overcome it in the best way possible for you, with your specific needs and circumstances. Winning is not always defined by permanently keeping your residence. Sometimes winning means remaining in the home for a significant length of time without paying to save money and make proper arrangements to move on gracefully. Other times victory involves capitalizing on opportunities to earn from the property by relocating. It can mean relieving yourself of debts, repairing damage to credit, or even just removing the stress of foreclosure from your life. Think of foreclosure as a game: learn the rules and strategies and then use them to your advantage to garner your best possible victory.

Keeping that insight in mind, it makes sense to illustrate a variety of different paths that can be taken and allow you to decide for yourself which direction makes the most sense for you. There is one option that is available to every homeowner in every state facing foreclosure, regardless of circumstances – obtaining more time in the home. The foreclosure process is designed to allow homeowners to obtain information and protect their rights should they so choose. Methods vary depending on which state you reside in, but options that are always available include verifying the debt, loan modification attempts, contesting the foreclosure in court, and bankruptcy (Chapters 7 and 13). Other tactics that are available in some states, or in certain situations, include mediation, contesting eviction proceedings, court appeals, and time-focused settlement agreements (relocation or "cash-for-keys" arrangements). Obviously if time is the primary objective, it is logical to use each method in chronological order and ensure that each step is drawn out maximally.

I believe that biding time in your home and using that time to save money is one of the wisest options available to homeowners facing foreclosure. Tens of thousands of dollars can be saved in the time available by not making mortgage payments and having that time available to properly plan your relocation saves a ton of stress and difficulty. It's important to understand that you are not hurting anyone by doing this, but rather are helping all parties concerned. Obviously it helps your family but beyond that your community is protected, your neighbors' equity positions are preserved, and your lender's assets are maintained. You staying there prevents vacancies and vandalism – two things that are prevalent in high foreclosure areas that both hurt the community and the lender as the property value of the home and the homes surrounding it will dwindle if abandoned.

If you don't want to stay in the home for emotional reasons, or if you have the opportunity to move on gracefully now, you have three options: deed-in-lieu, short sale, or just walking away. If you elect to just leave, make sure your state doesn't allow for deficiencies or that can come back to haunt you (See Appendix A). I would not recommend that tactic to anyone unless the emotional distress is unbearable to them. Deed-in-lieu means that the bank accepts the home in exchange for wiping out the mortgage and any deficiency. It's essentially calling it a draw, which a lot of people would likely be interested in. Unfortunately, banks want money, not properties, and therefore these agreements are hard to come by. A deed-in-lieu is impossible if you have multiple mortgages or liens.

A short sale is a sale of real property whereby the proceeds from the sale are less than the amount owed on the mortgage. Short sales must be accepted by the lender; they are not an automatic right to homeowners. If accepted by the lender, they agree to release the lien from the property for the property to be sold with clear title. If you have multiple mortgages or liens, each lien holder must all agree to the sale. Sometimes it is agreed that deficiencies will be waived, but usually deficiencies can still be pursued – this depends on the lender and the state your home is in. From 2007 to 2013 the Mortgage Forgiveness Debt Relief Act allowed you to write off deficiencies on your taxes, but that law has since expired. Short sales are expected to decrease significantly in light of that critical change to the tax code. Essentially, the lender holds most of the cards with regards to the terms of sale for the home.

Assuming the short sale is allowed, the property is sold in standard fashion just like any normal home sale. However, you receive no funds from the sale and credit reporting is at the sole discretion of your lender. Some banks report short sales more favorably than others, but there is no way to know in advance if the credit hit will be less or equivalent to foreclosure. Sometimes credit can be affected in a lesser capacity and for a lesser duration but other times the impact is the same or nearly as great as if the home was allowed to be foreclosed upon. Simply put, there is almost always an option available that will provide you with greater value than short selling your home.

Filing for bankruptcy is often touted to struggling homeowners as the easiest and cheapest solution for preventing foreclosure and getting their financial lives back on track – this is a deceiving notion. There are two types of bankruptcy the promoters of this tactic are referring to – Chapter 7 and Chapter 13 Bankruptcy – and each has its pros, cons, and appropriate uses. Both can be used to keep your home, buy time, or eliminate (or severely reduce) debts if utilized correctly. Used improperly, bankruptcy can have little to no effect besides a long-term credit hit.

Chapter 7 bankruptcy is the type most people think of when bankruptcy is mentioned. It can be useful to homeowners facing foreclosure, but only under specific conditions. Timing is everything with this type of bankruptcy. Once discharged by your trustee, Chapter 7 bankruptcy removes all personal debt except recent tax debt, child support, and student loans which is its primary benefit. If you have a large amount of personal debt that affects your ability to pay your mortgage, getting rid of all of those debts and reaffirming your mortgage might allow you to continue making your payments and avoid foreclosure. Should you be in that position, file as soon as you can so that you don't get behind in the first place. Another way Chapter 7 could possibly be used to keep your home is to file, list your mortgage as an unsecured debt, and wait for your lender to object. To complete an objection, it must prove that it owns the debt which can be difficult or impossible if the home was securitized. This is a bold strategy as it is not always effective so only try this if you also have other debts you need alleviated and know that your loan was securitized and assigned improperly.

The other time to use Chapter 7 Bankruptcy is when foreclosure proceedings are all but complete. This type of bankruptcy temporarily prevents foreclosure upon filing, generally for 30-90 days. That time is helpful in preventing eviction proceedings, but the real benefit to Chapter 7 bankruptcy as it pertains to foreclosure is that it can remove any liability for additional home loans, junior liens, and deficiency judgments. However, bankruptcy has its downsides as well – most notably destroyed credit and exemption limits. After filing, your credit will take a severe hit for several years. Additionally, each state has limits as to which and how much personal property can be claimed as exempt – everything else will be ordered to be sold by the Trustee to pay your creditors. So if you have valuable property, equity in your home, or significant cash reserves, be weary of that prior to filing. Exploiting the automatic stay to keep your home an extra month or two is just not worth it if that's the only reason you are considering filing. I've found in my experience that all too often people look at bankruptcy as an easy fix rather than the last resort it should be viewed as.

Chapter 7 bankruptcy should only be utilized when debts are overwhelming: liens, deficiencies, credit cards, personal judgments, and so on totaling an amount that is excessive as it compares to your income. Please note that not everyone can file for Chapter 7 Bankruptcy. If you have already done so within the last seven years or don't pass the means test (must have income below household median), you will not be approved for discharge. Should you elect to proceed with Chapter 7 Bankruptcy, you likely won't need an attorney so it will only cost a few hundred dollars in filing fees. If you would like an attorney to represent you, it will cost an extra one to two thousand dollars usually.

Chapter 13 Bankruptcy has its uses as well, but under entirely different circumstances. As described previously, some people use it as an avenue to obtain an Adversary Proceeding to contest foreclosure in the bankruptcy court venue. This is one valuable way to use Chapter 13. It can also be used to keep your home (permanently or temporarily), alleviate or reduce additional mortgages, and minimize unsecured debts.

Despite popular belief, Chapter 13 bankruptcy does not alleviate debts, it simply allows you to propose a reasonable payment plan to pay them off in lesser sums. Your plan must account for secured debts (i.e. mortgage or tax liens), living expenses, and sometimes Trustee fees and unsecured debts (i.e. credit cards or junior liens without equity to secure them). Secured debts must have full payments, so you will continue paying your first mortgage. Unsecured debts are paid based on remaining disposable income after secured debts and reasonable living expenses, not the amount of the debt. So, if you have only two hundred dollars per month after those expenses, only two hundred dollars per month will be allocated to your unsecured debts. Additionally, second and third mortgages that have no equity to support them being secured debts can be eliminated entirely.

Example: You have $4,000 per month in income and your secured debts and living expenses take up $3,800 of that, leaving you with $200 per month in disposable income. You have a $50,000 second mortgage that is unsecured due to an underwater first mortgage as well as $30,000 in credit card debt. Your payment plan is for three years so you have 36 total payments, or $7,200 total being paid to unsecured debt. Your credit card would be paid off for only $7,200 and your second mortgage would be stripped, assuming you completed the whole plan.

Upon filing, your Trustee will evaluate your income, living expenses, and debts, and then approve or deny your plan. Payment plans are for three or five year periods and if the full term payment plan is completed, your debts are considered paid in full. The exception to that is mortgages. For a mortgage loan, the Trustee will allocate funds to that debt each month but then after the three to five years the mortgage picks back up where it left off. This means that if income was insufficient to support the loan prior to the bankruptcy, it is likely that foreclosure proceedings will resume upon failure to keep the loan current after the bankruptcy is discharged. Further, trustees handling Chapter 13 petitions do not allow for significant disposable income – nearly all household income is allotted to creditors each month. Should the full payment plan term be completed, these allotments are dispersed to the creditors and the bankruptcy is discharged. The debtor has little to no control over their household budget; income is paid directly to the trustee to allocate as he or she sees fit. For this reason, the vast majority of Chapter 13 petitioners ultimately fail. One unforeseen expense can cripple the payment plan and then the bankruptcy is dismissed, all funds that have been paid to the Trustee are returned (less administrative costs), and creditors are free to pursue the debtor at their discretion.

Chapter 13 Bankruptcy can be useful in heavily reducing or removing unsecured debts and keeping your home if you can manage the duration of the payment plan. Most can't, so that's not often a viable option and I don't usually recommend that strategy. It can be useful for delaying the foreclosure significantly via the automatic stay (just like Chapter 7) and that stay will last for a few months. It can be delayed even further (another 1-3 months) by converting to a Chapter 7 later on so all told 4-6 months can be obtained via the bankruptcy route. A final downside to Chapter 13 is that it is complex so you will most likely need an attorney and that will cost at least a couple thousand dollars.

The ethics of delaying foreclosure proceedings can be debated (I believe it is positive for all but that's just my opinion) but the benefits to you as a homeowner are undeniable. Engaging in a time-extension strategy will allow you to gain financially via not making mortgage payments and obtain ample time to make relocation arrangements – the two primary concerns for most people facing foreclosure when they have no ability to permanently retain the home and no means to relocate. The effectiveness of such tactics are indisputable as well – the national average length of a foreclosure proceeding has doubled in just the past few years.[23] Of course the effectiveness varies from state to state, but regardless this strategy remains an option to all. The most important thing for you is to decide up front whether you wish to go after maximum time (to save money) or not. If you choose to pursue a time-extension strategy, start immediately upon missing your first payment – set aside all or most of what you normally would have paid. The worst thing you can do is wait until later and then decide you want time to save.

Depending on the methods utilized, the order in which they are used, individual circumstances, and the state in which the actions are taking place, other benefits may also be realized. Please keep in mind that this strategy is entirely ineffective if the low-cost living situation is not used to save money and find a place to relocate to gracefully. If you're not going to actually utilize the opportunity to accumulate savings, the effort and stress involved are simply not worthwhile. Obviously this tactic is more beneficial if you have higher mortgage payments as the savings will be greater while the legal procedure and cost remains identical.

Optimal results are realized when you understand that the likelihood of keeping the home is slim, realize that maximum time is the real victory, and yet proceed as if retaining the property is the sole objective. As late payment letters and calls begin coming in, respond to them and indicate that you are working to retain the property and are hoping to reinstate the loan. Once the Notice of Default is received, the next step is to submit a Qualified Written Request or Debt Verification Letter to the lender (There are many examples of these for each state online). These letters indicate that you are requesting, by right, a complete history of the loan to ensure that the proper party is foreclosing for the correct reasons. The effectiveness of such requests varies greatly from receiving an adequate response within 30 days (the allowed response time by law) to completely stalling the foreclosure process for an extended period of time. This variation is due to some lenders being unable to provide sufficient documentation for numerous reasons, ranging from a simple error resulting from multiple electronic transfers of the mortgage to blatantly fraudulent documents and everything in between. Sometimes, the responses to these requests can be highly beneficial in contesting foreclosure as lenders may indemnify themselves with regards to improper foreclosure proceedings. Regardless, after sending out the requests the best strategy is to simply wait for the lender to make the next move.

Submitting loan modification application(s) is usually the next strategic move. Generally, foreclosure proceedings are slowed down or halted to accommodate attempts to modify the loan, even when you don't qualify. Banks are overwhelmed with processing these applications, so even a denial takes significant time to receive. In some states, this time period also mandates the right to mediation. If such is the case in your state, take advantage. Mediation is a simple procedure whereby you will submit documentation (similar to loan modification) to the lender and then shortly thereafter both parties will meet with a mediator to attempt to resolve the matter amicably prior to the foreclosure. While mediation generally proves fruitless as far as resolution, sometimes it has positive results, and it certainly takes up more time.

The efforts indicated to this point will stall the initiation of foreclosure significantly but eventually it will commence. There are additional actions that can be taken at this juncture, but the variance between states expands greatly. In judicial states, you will receive a summons and complaint. A timely response to the complaint will prevent a judgment being obtained by default and force the case to proceed further. During this time motions, discovery requests, and a counter-complaint may be filed. Without knowing the details of an individual case it is impossible to make recommendations as to which, if any, of these documents should be filed and what they should or shouldn't contain within. Unless you are knowledgeable about what you should do, or have access to a cheap lawyer that does, and you know you have a good case, I wouldn't recommend pursuing the case much further as it will likely cost you more in legal fees than you will be able to save with the time gained.

Unless a significant issue of fact or a blatant misuse of the foreclosure process is discovered, ultimately a judgment will be issued. When facing a prospective judgment, it is wise to request a cash for keys arrangement whereby you will receive a monetary sum in exchange for dismissing the case and relocating upon a pre-determined date. In many cases (particularly FHA loans), lenders will agree to such an offer to avoid further litigation costs, make certain they will get the property they seek timely, and to prevent disgruntled residents from damaging the property prior to vacating. Of course, such an offer is not guaranteed to be accepted and if it is, the amount of time and money negotiated varies widely. Such variation largely depends on the case specifics and value of the home. Obviously a strong case or a highly valued property equates to a better deal. Regardless, you have nothing to lose by asking.

Non-judicial states can be a little bit trickier. The first thing to consider is whether or not your state has mandatory eviction proceedings after the auction of the home. If so, the option of whether to contest foreclosure via a Circuit Court complaint as Plaintiff prior to the auction or wait to contest in District Court as a Defendant arises. Opinions on this topic vary; sometimes a certain issue of fact pushes one of those options to the forefront, but other times it's likely irrelevant from a legal standpoint. That said, I tend to recommend the District Court route if available to avoid dual-tracking. This is a practice whereby the lender will still file a District Court action despite already litigating the same issues in Circuit Court. These cases are often difficult to joinder and therefore you end up fighting two battles simultaneously which adds up to more work and greater cost. Please note that even without dual-tracking, if the Circuit Court route is elected the time, effort, and monetary cost will likely be greater. In states where there is no necessity for an eviction action in District Court, the choice is made for you – if you want to contest, you must do so as Plaintiff.

Regardless of the decision to dispute the foreclosure as Plaintiff or Defendant, the arguments utilized must be sound and evidence sufficient in non-judicial states. Adherence to proper foreclosure process and ownership are not required to be proven by the foreclosing party – homeowners have the burden of proof. Many of the claims discussed previously to fight to keep the home can be used in this instance as well. The primary issue that will be encountered is the bank's attorneys arguing that you've "failed to state a claim" and pushing to dismiss the complaint summarily via a summary disposition motion. This can only be countered by compiling irrefutable evidence showing that something is wrong with the chain of title, the foreclosure procedure, or some other significant issue of fact. Otherwise, in most scenarios the case will be dismissed with prejudice fairly quickly, meaning that no further opportunity to contest the same foreclosure with the same argument(s) will be allowed in any court, though you can appeal for more time if you so choose. Please keep in mind that escrow payments may be ordered in which case you are likely better off letting it go and moving on as those payments would defeat the purpose of saving money. Should escrow be ordered, your best bet is to attempt to obtain a cash for keys arrangement or at least a pre-determined relocation date for peace of mind. If you do get by with no escrow, appealing can earn you a lot more time as higher courts tend to be much slower than lower ones.

Should all litigation efforts result in unfavorable rulings, eviction from the property will be promptly forthcoming. This is the time to move to the new housing accommodations you have been preparing for using some of the savings you've been accumulating. If you've done all of the steps outlined above, you should have been able to save up a hefty sum to move on with and likely won't experience much hardship in your relocation. Should you still not be quite ready to leave, you do have the final option of a bankruptcy stay as discussed previously, though without other debts to alleviate I do not recommend that.

Of course, the best foreclosure defense tactic is prevention. Obviously there is no undoing what has been done, but perhaps you can still get your finances together and avoid foreclosure. If not, measures can be taken to ensure that this situation is never encountered again. Proper money management strategies and sufficient levels of self-discipline are not commonplace in our society anymore. Most everyone aspires to a higher standard of living – that's great, but needs to be tempered with reason. The lost arts of savings and living within one's means need to be rediscovered and implemented.

There are many learning tools available to individuals looking to improve in these areas, but a great starting point is setting up three bank accounts – we'll call them Expense, Savings, and Luxury. Every time you receive any money (pay checks, bonuses, finding ten bucks on the floor, etc.), disperse that money as follows: 80% Expense, 10% Savings, and 10% Luxury. The Expense account is used for living expenses – bills, food, gas, entertainment, and so on. Obviously this implies adjusting living expenses to be compliant with the amount that goes into this account on a regular basis (i.e. not living on credit). The Savings account is for – you guessed it – saving money! Don't touch it; this money is for your future and emergencies. When you set this money aside and forget about it immediately upon receiving, it goes unnoticed most of the time. That said, life requires balance. If you are always saving, a part of your brain will be urging you to splurge because "hey, you've saved up $10,000, you deserve it!" Discipline can go a long way but eventually this part of the mind needs to be appeased or splurging is exactly what you'll do. That's what the Luxury account is for – you will save exactly the same amount as your Savings account, but this money is for treating yourself. Don't use it for things you would already do; this money is meant to fulfill the part of you that knows you deserve more in life. Go on vacation, buy the new TV you want, take your spouse to the best restaurant in town – whatever it is that you want to do that fits in the budget of your Luxury account, do it! An added bonus of both the Savings and Luxury accounts is the addiction factor. Seeing your account balance rise each month is addicting and so is experiencing the finer things in life. Use that motivation to then increase your means, while sticking to your money management plan. You'll be amazed at how fast your life changes when you control money rather than being controlled by it.

Be sure to read Appendix E and take a look at Appendix G as well. In Appendix E you'll find sixteen different case summaries. Each describes a unique situation regarding a foreclosure case. Real world examples embed ideas in your brain more effectively and each one imparts an important lesson – all summed up in one paragraph each. Appendix G contains some reading suggestions to boost your knowledge base on the many broad topics covered in this book. Don't worry – it's been kept brief so as to not overwhelm you… comprehending the most critical information trumps having a cursory understanding of a bunch of circumstantial data every time.

If you take nothing else away from this chapter, make it this: Everything will be fine! You are not defined by your home. Whether you are able or elect to keep your home, file bankruptcy, give your home up, or bide your time and save money, you will be OK. The only thing that can hurt you is you – if you let it cripple you emotionally or if you panic and become paralyzed to taking action, that's when you will have problems. Keep a cool head, make a choice, plan for that choice, and stick with it. Soon enough you will be back on track and all of the stress and heartache of foreclosure will be behind you.

Part 4: The Big Picture

The need to reform a clearly flawed system is obvious. What isn't as readily apparent is how exactly to go about that endeavor. Countless theories on the topic have emerged from homeowners, politicians, bankers, and economists over the past few years. A handful of individuals have procured some great ideas, but the vast majority of purported solutions have been unrealistic at best. These propositions primarily revolve around the concept of the federal government correcting the foreclosure crisis in one way or another. In theory, these concepts could be possible. However, most of these models are simply not realistic (or fair to lenders) and are therefore not being realized. The reality is that while the federal government is largely responsible for the construction of the housing crisis, it will likely play a much smaller role in its demolition.

The federal government oversees fifty states. Of those, only seventeen have a foreclosure rate that exceeds the national average at the time of this writing.[24] While that is surely a significant number, it is not the majority and therefore it wouldn't make sense to implement policy change affecting every state. Further, each state has its own unique foreclosure statutes and requirements so broad guidelines may benefit people in some states but have a negative or negligible impact in others. The biggest obstacle for the federal government in correcting the foreclosure epidemic is that to do so would require the admission that it helped to cause the problem and now has to reverse much of the fiscal policy alterations from the last century to fix it. Even if the government overcame all of the above, effective solutions would take an enormous amount of time to develop and implement – time that we don't have. The impact of incredible foreclosure rates has already been felt for seven years. There are millions of people suffering on account of the housing market right now and millions more will follow in the upcoming years. The problem isn't gone and isn't improving significantly, despite what the media would have the public believe – the time is now to take action. Uncle Sam isn't going to save us; it's up to the people to destroy this epidemic and protect one another, on an individual basis and at the local government level.

County governments actually have significant power to invoke positive change regarding foreclosures within their boundaries. However, most local politicians fail to acknowledge that the systems which have been relied upon for the past century are broken. County governments and local courts have become unconscious participants in an enterprise which fundamentally harms their citizens. The first step to overcoming foreclosure on a broad scale is awareness. Only when aware that there is a problem, and its people voice the need for help, can local governing bodies intervene. This entails educating public officials – perhaps via letters, speaking up at council meetings, presenting petitions signed by local residents, or publishing local news stories on the matter.

Foreclosure doesn't just negatively impact the people losing their homes. The entire region surrounding the homes is infected with vacancy issues, declining home values, financial institutions losing money, and dwindling property taxes which local governments rely on [and all benefit from]. Beyond the local predicaments, our national economy is drastically impacted by the foreclosure epidemic. To overcome the foreclosure crisis entirely would provide for an immense boost to the nation's broad financial picture as well as assert to all citizens that our government is behind us, a notion that is sadly no longer popular. The issue presented is not bipartisan, not left or right, simply moral and legal – any worthwhile politician should be willing to entertain facts and reasonable opinions offered on the subject.

Conceptual alteration is not easy to implement, but once realized opens up many opportunities for adaptation. Local government support allows for progress to take place in its natural order. Ironically, the next step is inaction. It is widely known (and unfortunately accepted) that wrongful foreclosures occur each and every day. Families are evicted from their homes unnecessarily by entities which may not have any rights to the properties or foreclosed without following the proper procedures. Citizens are not allowed to go around the legal system, so why should banks be above the law? Not every foreclosure is unjust, but a significant number are, and it's the duty of local government to protect its people from harm. The county cannot prevent foreclosure proceedings, but it can stop evictions. Nothing forces county Sheriffs to execute Writs of Eviction – they have complete authority as to whether or not they will enforce these orders. By not enforcing evictions, everything is put on hold whilst the problems get tidied up. Nobody is harmed – the homeowner is not forced to the streets and the lender does not lose its asset, it just can't take possession yet. This ability held by the county is very powerful. If no foreclosures can be completed until the mess is sorted out, it forces alterations to the system to ensure that every foreclosure is properly handled by the correct party.

With evictions halted, the county can then focus on changing policies to ensure that every foreclosure within its boundaries is conducted appropriately. This can be done in two relatively simple stages. The most common issue as far as improper foreclosure proceedings is inadequate notification, especially in non-judicial states. Horror stories have been heard across the nation of people first hearing of their pending foreclosure from outside sources or worse, finding out by seeing that a Notice to Vacate has been posted on their door. Of those that are given sufficient notice, few have any idea what their rights are or how to respond. Many individuals in this position are without resources to hire an attorney or consultants to assist them. Free resources are sometimes available, but are usually very limited and not easily found. Without awareness of the foreclosure, or knowledge of how to handle it when aware, inaction is the most common response. No reaction to foreclosure proceedings can lead to irreversible events which ultimately result in seizure of the homeowner's property. The majority of wrongful foreclosures could be prevented by fixing this one issue.

Banks are notorious for shortcomings in this aspect of foreclosure, whether their inadequacies are deliberate or due to incompetency. Thus, they should not be allowed to handle this procedure on their own.

Fortunately, by being proactive counties can take over this process and ensure equity to all. Mandating that all foreclosure notices must be processed by the county itself, rather than by the foreclosing party, ensures that a neutral third party is protecting all concerned. Going a step further, the county can make sure that each notice is accompanied by resources to explain the homeowner's rights, what they can do in response to the foreclosure, and advise them of local sources for assistance. Doing so makes certain that the county is aware of every pending foreclosure within its bounds, homeowners always receive proper notification, and local residents are aware of their rights. It also protects lenders from suits regarding improper foreclosure practices, so truly everybody wins. If criminals must be informed of their rights upon arrest, law-abiding homeowners certainly deserve nothing less.

The other prevalent issue pertaining to unjust foreclosure is the ownership position of the foreclosing party. It is not uncommon for the foreclosing party to lack proper standing to initiate such proceedings - this has been the topic of countless suits. In order to foreclose, the lender must be able to show a complete chain of title which ultimately results in its ownership of the property. This seems obvious, but nonetheless does not always happen. Sometimes these records cannot be procured. In more extreme cases, the documentation may be presented properly but is found to be fraudulent.

Once again, the county can easily solve this problem by taking things into its own hands. Simply requiring banks to file documentation with the county proving proper standing and ownership prior to initiating foreclosure proceedings is the starting point. From there, notifying all filers that any fraudulent documents that have been submitted will result in criminal prosecution completes the solution. With these two modest requirements in place, most improper foreclosures can be halted before they even get underway. As for the costs of applying these measures, the savings from processing less lawsuits and managing fewer abandoned properties resulting from these two issues would likely offset any expenses put towards their prevention.

The steps outlined above would go a long way towards mitigating the harmful effects of foreclosure, but do not eliminate them. As stated in Parts Two and Three, foreclosure cannot and should not be destroyed entirely. Foreclosures serve a necessary function when performed correctly and in the constructs of a healthy economy. The real problem is the housing market as a whole – values are incredibly inflated far beyond the [sadly] typical inflation rates that plague the economy of the United States. As long as prices remain fixed at such astronomical levels, the foreclosure epidemic will continue. It's straightforward math – income is not increasing at the same levels as housing expenses which leads to unsustainable living situations.

Numerous systems have been put in place by the federal government to re-align homeowner obligations (mortgage debt) with what the market value range should be for a given region. This is good but all efforts have largely failed because federal regulatory bodies prevent banks from renegotiating their secured debts on a large scale (and many can't even if they want to because the notes were securitized). Further, current policies incentify lenders to foreclosure rather than negotiate by making that the more profitable option. Principal reduction on mortgage notes is very rare for these reasons. The housing market can only deflate if average housing sale prices drop. Obviously this cannot occur if a large number of homes are in an upside down position and therefore unable to sell at what market value should be. The fastest and easiest solution to that problem: county governments using their constitutional right of eminent domain.

Eminent domain is the power to seize property for public use by a local or national government. In the United States, this concept is derived from colonial times when land could simply be taken because it was so abundant. When the Constitution of the United States was drafted, our Founding Fathers revised the notion slightly to ensure that no governing body could wrongfully seize property held by citizens without proper reparation. The 5th Amendment explicitly states "nor shall private property be taken for public use, without just compensation". This power held by the government is normally viewed negatively by the public, often for good reason. By utilizing a variation of classic eminent domain, it can be used by local government as a powerful tool for combating wrongful foreclosure and housing market rates.

> I highly recommend that you read Eminent Domain by Michael Sauvante to garner a more thorough grasp of this amazing concept. Mr. Sauvante has far greater expertise on this subject than I and has been kind enough to make this book freely available to our readers by visiting *http://www.eminent-domain.us* and downloading it (PDF). The book is also available in print and Kindle format from Amazon.com.

Hostility from citizens regarding eminent domain will likely dissipate with the addition of this small, but powerful, adjustment to the traditional use of this power. Rather than seizing real property (the home) from the title holder (homeowner) in exchange for a monetary sum, the county can use eminent domain to seize the personal property (mortgage) from the mortgage holder (bank). The just compensation to the mortgage holder would be negotiated between the county and the bank – this is how market values get realigned with real prices. This is likely beneficial to the lender as it would generally recoup greater sums than those earned from processing a foreclosure which ultimately end up getting sold at drastically reduced prices via REO sales. Further, the bank would get its funds much faster and without the need for such extensive efforts to obtain that money. The county can exercise this right to property seizure when a foreclosure is imminent; it would know when this is happening by simply following the steps laid forth previously (foreclosing parties filing with the county). The process of eminent domain supersedes foreclosure proceedings in the courts as a Constitutional right; thus the foreclosure process would be terminated and the county would be left to hold the mortgage as the bank had previously.

Once that process has been completed, the county is able to renegotiate the loan with the homeowner, free of any regulations or contrasting objectives. The modification to the loan could factor in any number of conditions including, but not limited to, the price paid by the county and the ability of the homeowner to pay. This freedom to openly negotiate pricing is the key to correcting the housing market.

Obviously this sophisticated process goes beyond the normal expertise of county governments, but that's OK – counties already employ numerous private sector enterprises to assist with their endeavors. It would not be difficult to utilize the services of organizations in the community to implement this system under the oversight of local government. The primary skills that would need to be contracted are negotiation abilities (to work with both banks and homeowners) and finance specialties (to determine new loan terms).

Such a system would allow homeowners to stay in their homes under revised loans that could be maintained adequately. Should a homeowner not be able to afford even the modified loan terms, foreclosure would remain an inevitable course of action. While unfortunate for those people, the facts remain that with this process they would have been given every opportunity to retain their home and the possibility for wrongful eviction would be extremely low. In the rare case that a homeowner was wronged, they would preserve the right to contest. Even under those circumstances, this type of foreclosure is far better for the community as a whole than the current norm as the county would have the ability to ensure that the foreclosed homeowners had proper guidance, the properties were maintained well, and vacancies were quickly filled. Beyond that, when the property was resold to a new member of the community, the price would be aligned with proper market values, rather than inflated ones.

By resolving its own local foreclosure and housing market problems in this fashion, counties are able to procure results that the federal government has not been able to. The best part is that every party involved benefits and is protected. One question remains though: How do these homes get paid for by the county? Governments have various tools at their disposal for obtaining financing for projects. If these ventures are revenue generating, they can be self-sufficient and not require any further funding. Under the system described above, the county would be purchasing mortgages which have revenue-generating capability as well as equity from the secured assets. This puts the county in a favorable position for borrowing funds. However, this would put the county in a highly leveraged position, meaning that its broad-scope capabilities would be limited considerably. Further, funds would still be necessary to perform these operations which would have to be derived from tax dollars – not possible for many counties in which simply balancing the budget is difficult enough. Most counties do have substantial net assets though, which leads to a solution of this problem as well as radically improved financial resources for counties, local businesses, and their citizens.

Almost every state's laws allow for counties and the state itself to obtain a bank charter from its state as a DBA of the government body. This form of banking is called public banking, which means that the local government owns the bank rather than private investors or Wall Street corporations. The purpose of a public bank is to allow the county or state to take advantage of the inherent legal rights of banking institutions for the good of its citizens. Though an overly simplistic description of banking operations, banks are able to lend so widely because they can literally create credit money based off of the assets they have on the books. The ratio of assets to credit varies, but as a general rule is roughly 1:10.[25] The ability to leverage assets at such an incredible rate allows for a typical county or state to amplify its financial reach immensely. An average county has at least $100 million in net assets[26]; some have less, and many have much more. Therefore, by utilizing a public banking system, a typical county could produce credit of up to $1 billion – far more than it would need to correct any foreclosure-related issues via eminent domain. The excess credit lines would not have to be used, but could be made available to local citizens for business loan guarantees (loans originated by local private-sector banks) or utilized for other purposes used to enhance the community.

Counties have the ability, through the creation of a public bank, to generate all of that credit without selling any of their assets which have been accumulated by tax dollars over long periods. Obviously this form of monetizing assets is far superior to the current method used by many counties when in need of cash – useable funds are usually generated by selling off assets, often for cents on the dollar. There are many different types of banks; not all operate as we usually think of with checking accounts, savings accounts, and the like. A public bank can act similarly to a Federal Reserve Bank but only for its local region, meaning that it provides or guarantees loans for local private-sector banks to be used for the community, but is not open for general public use. By acting in this fashion, a public bank can nurture its local economy without detracting from resident banks.

Sure, the concept sounds fantastic on paper, but can this realistically be implemented? Has any governing body actually put a system such as this into use? One state has, and by no coincidence it also happens to be the only solvent state in the union.[27] North Dakota shows every state how it's done and the housing market isn't the only benefactor, though with only 461 foreclosures in all of 2013 that aspect of the economy is clearly healthy. To put that in perspective, *more than four times that many foreclosures were completed in Florida per week during the same year.*[28] The least visited state in the country boasts the lowest unemployment rate (2.6%) of any state and has the highest GDP per capita as well.[29][30] North Dakota is consistently rated the best run state within the union and much of its economic success can be attributed to the Bank of North Dakota, the state's own central bank. "Much of its economic success" may be an understatement – profits from the Bank of North Dakota represent the single largest income source for the state of North Dakota[31], surpassing even oil which is generally assumed to be its leading source of revenue. This state uses its public bank to achieve such fantastic economic results, yet without harming other privately held banks at all. In fact, North Dakota has the most local banks per capita of any state, and not one has gone insolvent in over ten years.[32]

The concept of public banking has been adopted by a few local governments in Europe and it has been largely successful there as well (particularly in Germany). It is time that the other states and counties in the union take note of this obviously superior economic model and implement it in their regions. By doing so, local governments and everyday people can overcome many economic difficulties, including the foreclosure epidemic, without any need for federal intervention.

Economic repair, especially as it pertains to foreclosure rates and the housing market, begins and ends with local government. That is not to say, however, that the federal government can't or shouldn't play a role. In particular, three specific actions that can only be completed by the federal government should be taken to ensure the success of local public banks as well as the general health of our nation's economy. The first two go hand in hand and pertain specifically to local public banks. Currently, it is federal law that every newly formed bank must join the Federal Deposit Insurance Corporation (FDIC) program. The FDIC was created to protect private citizens with depositors' insurance – a noble cause. This entity insures bank accounts up to $250,000 and also retains the right to seize banks' assets if they don't follow FDIC guidelines. This makes perfect sense in private banking – people should be protected. However, these rules make no sense for a public bank that does not take deposits, particularly because the bank's assets would be the county's assets and therefore the FDIC would have the ability to seize all assets of a county which clearly makes no sense. Though such action is unlikely, it is possible and should be protected against sooner rather than later. The federal government could solve this very simply by granting an exemption to the FDIC program for public banks only.

Remember the Bank Holding Company Act (BHCA) from Part 1 of this book? The second thing the federal government could do to assist with economic repair via this logical plan is to grant an exemption for public banks from this Act. Bank holding companies are defined as entities which own banks but do not engage in banking themselves (i.e. the county or state in this case if they elected to not operate as a direct DBA of the state).

This could be a problem for public banks ran by local government because the BHCA allows for regulatory oversight from the Federal Reserve for all bank holding companies. Such oversight is unwarranted for public banks because they do not engage in the activities that the Act is meant to protect against. Further, this regulation does not come from the federal government itself but rather a central bank that is wholly owned and controlled by twelve regional Federal Reserve banks which are private corporations. Thus, by not granting such an exemption, counties could ultimately end up being regulated by those twelve corporations which destroys the purpose of the public bank. If granted, public banks could operate free of such oversight and with any corporate structure the state or county saw fit. As of now, counties wishing to implement a public banking system must have it operate as a DBA of the local governing body to avoid such regulations.

The final step for the federal government doesn't strictly pertain to local public banks or the foreclosure crisis, but the entire economy of the United States. This step would require time, a willingness to admit fault, and a push from individual citizens and local governments. However, this third stage is equally straightforward and logical based on the results we've seen from current policies – simply reverse what got us to this point over the last century. It may be easier said than done, but if this country has proven one thing it's that anything is possible. Our economy can be made reasonably whole and strong once more solely on the backs of the states, counties, and individual citizens of this nation. But if the United States government took that extra step, there's no telling what possibilities may unfold for our country economically.

If you watch or read any economic news, housing reports, or finance journals it will quickly become clear that nobody has any real idea based on facts as to what the future holds for the housing market. This is largely due to a severe lack of accurate data that encompasses the entire housing market. Traditional housing price and sale data is no longer sufficient due to so many homes being underwater, in default, in the foreclosure process, or abandoned. Information is further distorted because of an expansive "shadow inventory" of foreclosure homes, meaning properties that are heavily in default but for some reason the lender has not foreclosed yet. What ends up happening is specific data is skewed to favor the opinion of the writer or speaker and in doing so, almost any point can be made to seem accurate. Some have the public believing that the housing market crisis is almost over. A few are so bold as to state that foreclosures and housing prices will be at healthy levels within a mere couple of years. Others point to the other end of the spectrum stating that the foreclosure crisis has no end in sight and the American public will be facing housing issues for years to come. I'll leave the macroeconomic arguments to the economists and other more qualified individuals and take a more anecdotal approach.

Regardless of the severity of the foreclosure epidemic in upcoming years, two things are certain – it's not gone yet and even if it were, our economy as a whole is unstable at best on a national scale. In regards to the former, anybody that resides in or visits an area which has been especially plagued with foreclosure issues can clearly see that the problem is not fixed – many communities have been and remain devastated. Should the foreclosure crisis expand as some say, it will only get worse for those areas and potentially others. If it does dwindle instead, the current epidemic is so vast and of such great magnitude that there is little doubt that complete recovery will take a substantial length of time.

The housing market is but one aspect in the intricate expanse of the United States economy as a whole. It goes beyond the scope of this book to discuss, but significant issues that affect us all include declining labor markets, poor budget control (for individuals and governing bodies), outrageous financial leveraging (*credit derivatives of the U.S. alone exceeds total world currency by more than tenfold*)[33], and excessive taxation (to cover a mismanaged federal budget with a consistent deficit). Focusing on problems does nobody any good; solutions should always be the primary focus. To that end, individuals should concentrate on what is within their immediate control first and then encourage others to do the same. Defend yourself and get back on track with regards to your home, make sure your personal finances are managed properly, and then be proactive with your local government. Systemic change begins with individuals, extends into local government, and then expands into federal government. Each of us hold the power, and has the civic duty, to do our part to ensure our nation's economy flourishes once more rather than deteriorates.

Share the Wealth

I'm a big believer in paying it forward. Knowledge is power and what better way to use that power than to help others? This book has given you all of the necessary ammunition to battle foreclosure and protect yourself. It has also provided you with the insight needed to change the system as a whole, starting with your community. I'm very humbled and grateful that you have read this far, giving me the opportunity to give you this final message that in my mind is one of the most important one in this book.

Everyone constantly preaches that they wish the world was a better place. Start with you being better. Take your situation from poor to excellent. In doing so you gain self-respect and admiration, the ultimate reward. But then you have the duty to make sure that others have that same opportunity. You must enlighten yourself to light up the world. Too many individuals have altered the course of the future by starting in their own back yard to argue against that possibility.

Always remember that it's not you versus the world – you are part of that world. Don't attack the government and banking systems for revenge; holding that anger in your heart only hurts you and those around you. Defend yourself out of love for yourself and your family. Change the system out of respect for your country and your people. And make sure that you encourage as many others to join that cause as possible.

Appendices

I. Appendix A: Outline of foreclosure laws for each state

II. Appendix B: Listing of common loan servicers' contact information

III. Appendix C: Listing of known robo-signers

IV. Appendix D: Listing of major foreclosure mills in each state

V. Appendix E: Sample Case Studies

VI. Appendix F: Functional Glossary

VII. Appendix G: Suggested Reading

Please note that no complete case outlines or drafts of various defenses have been provided as it would be irresponsible to display template cases that will only be applicable to very specific circumstances without knowing the facts of the case. All court records are public however and therefore by simply going to your local courthouse, every document will be available for your review. Many counties also have these documents available as an online resource for your convenience. Federal case documents can be obtained from www.Pacer.gov but a registered login is required to gain access to that resource.

Appendix A: Outline of Foreclosure Laws in Each State

The material contained below provides information regarding foreclosure laws in each state. Please remember that each state's laws remain summarized and therefore do not contain every detail. The statutes cited for each state do reveal all and therefore should be referred to for any questions. These summaries only cover the most common foreclosure method in each state and in some cases there are alternate methods allowed by law. Make sure you understand that laws do change all the time and they always remain subject to interpretation by courts.

Alabama	
General foreclosure type	Non-Judicial
Estimated Process Period When Uncontested*	50-75 days
Sale Publish Period	21 days publishing; must start 30 days prior to sale
Time to Respond	N/A
Loan Reinstatement Options	N/A
Loan Redemption Options	1 year (only available if surrendered to new owner within the 10 day written eviction notice)
Deficiency Judgments	May be obtained by filing a lawsuit
Eviction Procedure	Entitled to a written 10 day notice to leave before eviction proceedings may be brought
Foreclosure Statutes	Ala. Code §§ 35-10-1 to 35-10-30, 6-5-247 to 6-5-256

*These estimates do not include the pre-foreclosure time prior to acceleration of the loan or any applicable redemption period. Please note that these time frames may vary substantially depending on specific circumstances.

Alaska	
General foreclosure type	Non-Judicial
Estimated Process Period When Uncontested	105 days
Sale Publish Period	65 days publishing; must be 90 days before sale
Time to Respond	N/A
Loan Reinstatement Options	Available any time prior to sale
Loan Redemption Options	N/A (1 year if judicially foreclosed)
Deficiency Judgments	Not allowed
Eviction Procedure	New owner must give former owner a notice to leave. New owner may file civil lawsuit to gain possession.
Foreclosure Statutes	Alaska Stat. § 34.20.070 et seq.

Arizona	
General foreclosure type	Non-Judicial
Estimated Process Period When Uncontested	90+ days
Sale Publish Period	Must be published for 4 consecutive weeks and be posted on the property 20 days prior to sale. Publishing must start at least 90 days prior to sale.
Time to Respond	N/A
Loan Reinstatement Options	Available up until day of sale.
Loan Redemption Options	N/A
Deficiency Judgments	Not allowed for single or two-family residences.
Eviction Procedure	New owner must demand the occupant to vacate in writing (no specific time frame in statute). If the occupant doesn't leave, new owner must get an eviction judgment in court.
Foreclosure Statutes	Ariz. Rev. Stat. §§ 33-721 to 33-749, 33-801 to 33-821, 12-1281 to 12-1283, 12-1566

Arkansas	
General foreclosure type	Both, but non-judicial is favored
Estimated Process Period When Uncontested	70 days
Sale Publish Period	Must publish for 4 consecutive weeks at least 30 days prior to sale. Must also send certified mail notice to homeowner 30 days prior to sale.
Time to Respond	N/A
Loan Reinstatement Options	Available up until date of sale
Loan Redemption Options	N/A (1 year if judicially foreclosed)
Deficiency Judgments	Allowed for up to the market value of the home. To obtain a suit must be filed within 1 year.
Eviction Procedure	Arkansas law does not specify a procedure
Foreclosure Statutes	Ark. Code Ann. §§ 18-50-101 to 18-50-116

California	
General foreclosure type	Non-Judicial
Estimated Process Period When Uncontested	120-140 days
Sale Publish Period	Lenders must personally contact (or meet the requirements for attempting to contact) homeowners to explore options for avoiding foreclosure 30 days before recording the notice of default. All homeowners get a 90-day notice of default and a 20-day notice of sale.
Time to Respond	N/A
Loan Reinstatement Options	Allowed up to 5 days prior to sale
Loan Redemption Options	N/A
Deficiency Judgments	Not allowed
Eviction Procedure	New owner must give occupant a 3 day notice to leave. If occupant doesn't leave, new owner must file an unlawful detainer lawsuit to evict.
Foreclosure Statutes	Cal. Civ. Code §§ 2923.5, 2924 to 2924I

Please note that the California Homeowners Bill of Rights, enacted January 1, 2013, grants homeowners more rights and remedies regarding foreclosures including protection against dual tracking and robo-signing, among others.

Colorado	
General foreclosure type	Non-Judicial. The foreclosing party must file proof of ownership and the homeowner's default with a public trustee prior to the foreclosure proceedings. The mortgage holder must separately obtain a court order authorizing the sale and give the public trustee a copy of the order prior to the sale date.
Estimated Process Period When Uncontested	165-180 days
Sale Publish Period	At least 30 days after default and at least 30 days prior to recording the Notice of Election and Demand the borrower must be served with information on how to prevent foreclosure. Within 10 days after the Notice of Election and Demand has been recorded, and 110-125 days before the scheduled sale, the public trustee must mail notice to the homeowner.
Time to Respond	N/A
Loan Reinstatement Options	Available until 15 days prior to the sale or the day before the sale if written notice of an intention to reinstate the loan is given to the foreclosing party 15 days prior to the sale.
Loan Redemption Options	N/A
Deficiency Judgments	Allowed
Eviction Procedure	The lender must make a demand for possession. If the borrower does not vacate, then the lender must file a lawsuit to evict.
Foreclosure Statutes	Colo. Rev. Stat. §§ 38-38-100.3 to 38-38-114

Connecticut	
General foreclosure type	Judicial
Estimated Process Period When Uncontested	90 days (no judgment can be entered for at least 90 days after the date of service of the foreclosure complaint)
Sale Publish Period	N/A
Time to Respond	After the foreclosing party files the foreclosure lawsuit, homeowner has 20 to 30 days to respond (depending on service method).
Loan Reinstatement Options	N/A
Loan Redemption Options	Court determined
Deficiency Judgments	May be obtained within 30 days after the redemption period expires.
Eviction Procedure	Foreclosure judgment comes with ordered sale and order of ejectment.
Foreclosure Statutes	Conn. Gen. Stat. §§ 49-1 to 49-31i

Delaware	
General foreclosure type	Judicial
Estimated Process Period When Uncontested	150-180 days
Sale Publish Period	Varies but generally about 60 days. Order to show cause must be posted in ten places, served on homeowner by sheriff, and published 2 weeks prior to sale.
Time to Respond	20 days from date of service of complaint
Loan Reinstatement Options	N/A
Loan Redemption Options	Available until court confirms sale
Deficiency Judgments	Allowed (must file separate suit)
Eviction Procedure	Must file suit at least 5 days after sale (for a hearing within 30 days). Can defend at hearing but if lost or not challenged, court will issue an eviction.
Foreclosure Statutes	Del. Code Ann. tit. 10, § 5061

Florida	
General foreclosure type	Judicial
Estimated Process Period When Uncontested	120-180 days
Sale Publish Period	Foreclosing party must publish notice of sale for 2 consecutive weeks at least 5 days before sale. Local courts have power to stay proceedings for mediation.
Time to Respond	21 days from date of personal service or 31 days from publishing date
Loan Reinstatement Options	Available prior to acceleration of loan. May be available for high-cost loans prior to sale.
Loan Redemption Options	Court determined. Generally not allowed.
Deficiency Judgments	Allowed if homeowner is personally served in foreclosure lawsuit. Court has flexibility regarding amount of deficiency. Foreclosing party may also file a separate lawsuit for breach of contract against homeowner for a deficiency.
Eviction Procedure	Generally included in the foreclosure judgment for a 24 hour relocation period. If not complied with, a Sheriff executes the order.
Foreclosure Statutes	Fla. Stat. Ann. §§ 701.10, 45.031 and 45.0315

Please note that Florida foreclosure laws are among the most complex and difficult to understand. Consulting with a local attorney is highly recommended.

Georgia	
General foreclosure type	Non-Judicial
Estimated Process Period When Uncontested	35-45 days (longer for high cost loans)
Sale Publish Period	Mail to homeowner 30 days prior to sale
Time to Respond	N/A
Loan Reinstatement Options	High cost loans may be reinstated up until date of sale
Loan Redemption Options	N/A
Deficiency Judgments	Sometimes allowed. Court must determine whether the sale was at a fair market value prior to issuing a judgment.
Eviction Procedure	New owner may immediately seek a court order to evict the occupants
Foreclosure Statutes	Ga. Code Ann. §§ 44-14-160 to 44-14-191

Hawaii	
General foreclosure type	Both. Judicial favored recently (this chart indicates the judicial method)
Estimated Process Period When Uncontested	180 days
Sale Publish Period	3 consecutive weeks with the 3rd being at least 2 weeks prior to the sale
Time to Respond	20 days from the date of service
Loan Reinstatement Options	N/A
Loan Redemption Options	N/A
Deficiency Judgments	Allowed for judicial foreclosures only
Eviction Procedure	Must get a judgment of eviction to remove occupant
Foreclosure Statutes	Haw. Rev. Stat. §§ 667-1 to 667-46, 667-A to 667-AC

Idaho	
General foreclosure type	Non-Judicial
Estimated Process Period When Uncontested	150 days
Sale Publish Period	Must provide 120-day notice of default and sale before the date set for sale, make additional attempts to personally serve notice of sale, post notice of sale on property at least 30 days before the sale, and publish notice of sale over 4 consecutive weeks at least 30 days before sale.
Time to Respond	The notice of default and sale must be accompanied by a modification request form which homeowners may respond to (and should). The lender must respond to a request for modification within 45 days and may not proceed to a foreclosure sale until it has responded to the modification request.
Loan Reinstatement Options	Available for 115 days from receipt of sale notice
Loan Redemption Options	N/A
Deficiency Judgments	May be obtained in a lawsuit brought within 3 months after sale. Deficiency limited by market value at time of sale.
Eviction Procedure	New owner has to wait 10 days after sale and then file suit for eviction, with hearing to be heard within 12 days of filing.
Foreclosure Statutes	Idaho Code §§ 45-1502 to 45-1515

Illinois	
General foreclosure type	Judicial
Estimated Process Period When Uncontested	240-300 days
Sale Publish Period	After court issues a judgment of foreclosure, notice must be published 3 times between 45 and 7 days before sale.
Time to Respond	20-30 days, depending on type of service
Loan Reinstatement Options	Available up to 90 days after service of complaint
Loan Redemption Options	Available for 7 months after the complaint is served or 3 months after foreclosure judgment entered, whichever is later.
Deficiency Judgments	Can be sought as part of foreclosure suit
Eviction Procedure	Generally the court orders occupants to leave within 30 days after sale
Foreclosure Statutes	735 Ill. Comp. Stat §§ 5/15-1501 to 5/15-1512

Indiana	
General foreclosure type	Judicial
Estimated Process Period When Uncontested	240 days
Sale Publish Period	Notice of sale must be published at least 30 days before the scheduled sale. Notice of sale must be published once a week for 3 consecutive weeks. Foreclosing party must give homeowner 30 days' notice before filing foreclosure complaint.
Time to Respond	20-30 days depending on service type. Home cannot be sold for at least 90 days after filing of the complaint.
Loan Reinstatement Options	Available prior to sale for high-cost loans
Loan Redemption Options	Available any time before the final judgment
Deficiency Judgments	Allowed if authorized by loan or written agreement
Eviction Procedure	New owner must give occupants 5 day notice to leave and then ask court for order of eviction.
Foreclosure Statutes	Ind. Code §§ 32-30-10-1 to 32-30-10-14, 32-29-1-1 to 32-29-1-11, 32-29-7-1 to 32-29-7-14

Iowa	
General foreclosure type	Judicial
Estimated Process Period When Uncontested	150 days
Sale Publish Period	Foreclosing party must mail notice of default to homeowner at least 30 days before filing suit. Must post and publish notice 4 weeks prior to sale.
Time to Respond	20-30 days depending on service type
Loan Reinstatement Options	Available until 30 days after receipt of notice of default
Loan Redemption Options	1 year
Deficiency Judgments	Allowed
Eviction Procedure	Must file for separate eviction order
Foreclosure Statutes	Iowa Code §§ 654.1 to 654.26, 628.26, 628.27

Kansas	
General foreclosure type	Judicial
Estimated Process Period When Uncontested	120-150 days
Sale Publish Period	After court issues a foreclosure judgment, foreclosing party must publish a notice of sale at least 3 times with the last publication between 7 and 14 days prior.
Time to Respond	20 days personal service; 41 days if only service is publication/posting
Loan Reinstatement Options	N/A
Loan Redemption Options	3 months if less than 1/3 of loan was paid off prior to foreclosure. Court may extend this period by another 3 months if homeowner can show sufficient hardship. 12 months if more than 1/3 of loan was paid off prior to foreclosure.
Deficiency Judgments	Allowed if court confirms that the price paid for property at sale is reasonable market value
Eviction Procedure	Must file a petition for ejection which usually takes 1-2 weeks to get an order
Foreclosure Statutes	Kan. Stat. Ann. § 60-2410

Kentucky	
General foreclosure type	Judicial
Estimated Process Period When Uncontested	120-150 days
Sale Publish Period	When court issues a foreclosure judgment, foreclosing party must publish notice for 3 consecutive weeks with the last one being at least 15 days prior to sale.
Time to Respond	20 days
Loan Reinstatement Options	N/A except under specific circumstances
Loan Redemption Options	1 year (if sale amount is less than 2/3 of its appraised value)
Deficiency Judgments	Allowed (homeowner must be personally served complaint or not respond)
Eviction Procedure	10 day writ of possession issued by court
Foreclosure Statutes	Ky. Rev. Stat. Ann. §§ 426.525 to 426.720

Louisiana	
General foreclosure type	Judicial. Oftentimes the process is reduced to an "executory" proceeding, which operates like a non-judicial foreclosure. In the mortgage document, the homeowner will typically have agreed to a clause whereby he or she "confessed to judgment" in case of a default. Upon default, the lender will file a complaint with the mortgage as an exhibit. Usually, the court will then order the property to be sold unless the homeowner appeals or files suit.
Estimated Process Period When Uncontested	180 days
Sale Publish Period	Notice of sale is contained in the complaint which is served by being posted on the property. Once court issues foreclosure judgment, notice of seizure is published at least twice and not less than 3 days after the debtor has been served.
Time to Respond	Usually N/A (executory proceeding)
Loan Reinstatement Options	N/A
Loan Redemption Options	N/A
Deficiency Judgments	Allowed
Eviction Procedure	No notice required. Sheriff can execute immediately after sale.
Foreclosure Statutes	La. Code Civ. Proc. Ann. Arts. 3721 to 3753, 2631 to 2772

Maine	
General foreclosure type	Judicial
Estimated Process Period When Uncontested	240 days
Sale Publish Period	After the court issues a foreclosure judgment, must publish sale for 3 consecutive weeks. Sale must be held 30 to 45 days after date of first publication. Lender must also mail a notice of sale at least 30 days before sale date.
Time to Respond	20 days
Loan Reinstatement Options	At court's discretion. Lender may allow reinstatement any time prior to sale.
Loan Redemption Options	90 days from date of judgment (may be extended by appealing decision)
Deficiency Judgments	Allowed (some limitations)
Eviction Procedure	Not specifically outlined in statute so likely to have to obtain a court order for eviction
Foreclosure Statutes	Me. Rev. Stat. Ann. tit. 14, §§ 6101 to 6325

Maryland	
General foreclosure type	Non-Judicial, but court must approve
Estimated Process Period When Uncontested	45-60 days
Sale Publish Period	Lender must serve notice of intent to foreclose at least 45 days before sale date by certified mail. Must also publish for at least 3 consecutive weeks (with last one at least 1 week prior to sale) and serve a final notice 10-30 days prior to sale.
Time to Respond	N/A
Loan Reinstatement Options	Allowed up until day prior to sale
Loan Redemption Options	N/A
Deficiency Judgments	Available if requested by supervising court after the sale
Eviction Procedure	Not specifically outlined in statute so likely to have to obtain a court order for eviction
Foreclosure Statutes	Md. Code Ann. [Real Prop.] §§ 7-105 to 7-105.8

Massachusetts	
General foreclosure type	Both; non-judicial is favored
Estimated Process Period When Uncontested	75-105 days
Sale Publish Period	Prior to acceleration, must give a 90 day written notice of ability to reinstate. After that, must send certified mail notice 14 days prior to sale and publish the sale for 3 consecutive weeks.
Time to Respond	N/A
Loan Reinstatement Options	Available 90 days from default
Loan Redemption Options	N/A
Deficiency Judgments	Can be obtained in separate lawsuit if a notice of intent to seek a deficiency is included in notice of sale
Eviction Procedure	Must obtain separate court order
Foreclosure Statutes	Mass. Gen. Laws Ch. 244, § 14, 35A

Michigan	
General foreclosure type	Non-Judicial
Estimated Process Period When Uncontested	60-90 days
Sale Publish Period	Must send notice of mediation opportunity prior to initiating foreclosure proceedings. After that, must be published for 4 consecutive weeks prior to sale and posted to door of home at least 14 days prior to sale.
Time to Respond	N/A
Loan Reinstatement Options	N/A
Loan Redemption Options	6 months. Can be 12 months under certain circumstances or reduced to 1-3 months if home is deemed abandoned.
Deficiency Judgments	Allowed if lender buys property at sale
Eviction Procedure	Must get separate order for eviction
Foreclosure Statutes	Mich. Comp. Laws §§ 600.3101 to 600.3180, 600.3201 to 600.3285

Minnesota	
General foreclosure type	Non-Judicial
Estimated Process Period When Uncontested	90 days
Sale Publish Period	Must serve notice of sale on homeowner at least 4 weeks before the sale and must publish the notice 6 weeks before the sale.
Time to Respond	N/A
Loan Reinstatement Options	Available until date of sale
Loan Redemption Options	6 months
Deficiency Judgments	Not allowed with non-judicial foreclosure
Eviction Procedure	Must get separate eviction order (have to wait until 2 months after redemption period expires)
Foreclosure Statutes	Minn. Stat. §§ 580.01 to 580.30

Mississippi	
General foreclosure type	Non-Judicial
Estimated Process Period When Uncontested	60-90 days
Sale Publish Period	Foreclosing party must publish notice of sale 3 consecutive weeks before sale date and post notice on the courthouse door. No notice need be served to homeowner.
Time to Respond	N/A
Loan Reinstatement Options	Available until date of sale
Loan Redemption Options	N/A
Deficiency Judgments	May be obtained if filed within 1 year of sale. Court may deny deficiency.
Eviction Procedure	Not specifically outlined in statute so likely to have to obtain a court order for eviction
Foreclosure Statutes	Miss. Code. Ann. §§ 89-1-55 to 89-1-59

Missouri	
General foreclosure type	Non-Judicial
Estimated Process Period When Uncontested	45-60 days
Sale Publish Period	Must send certified mail notice 20 days prior to sale
Time to Respond	N/A
Loan Reinstatement Options	N/A
Loan Redemption Options	1 year (homeowner must give lender a notice of intent to redeem at least 10 days before sale and the lender must buy the property at foreclosure sale)
Deficiency Judgments	Allowed (must file separate suit)
Eviction Procedure	Must give 1 month written notice
Foreclosure Statutes	Mo. Rev. Stat. §§ 443.290 to 443.453

Montana	
General foreclosure type	Both; non-judicial favored
Estimated Process Period When Uncontested	60-120 days
Sale Publish Period	Must personally serve occupants with a 30-day notice before sale. Must also post notice in 5 places prior to 30 days prior to sale.
Time to Respond	N/A
Loan Reinstatement Options	Available up until day of sale
Loan Redemption Options	1 year judicial; N/A non-judicial
Deficiency Judgments	N/A
Eviction Procedure	Generally need a court order to evict
Foreclosure Statutes	Mont. Code Ann. §§ 71-1-221 to 71-1-235 and §§ 71-1-301 to 71-1-321

Nebraska	
General foreclosure type	Both; non-judicial is favored
Estimated Process Period When Uncontested	150 days
Sale Publish Period	Must record notice of default 30 days prior to acceleration. Notice of sale must be published once a week for 5 consecutive weeks with last one 10-30 days prior.
Time to Respond	N/A
Loan Reinstatement Options	Available up to 30 days from default
Loan Redemption Options	N/A
Deficiency Judgments	May be obtained in a separate suit within 3 months of sale
Eviction Procedure	Not specifically outlined in statute so likely need to obtain a court order for eviction
Foreclosure Statutes	Neb. Rev. Stat. §§ 76-1005, 76-1018

Nevada	
General foreclosure type	Both; non-judicial favored
Estimated Process Period When Uncontested	90-150 days
Sale Publish Period	Must give homeowner a 3 month notice of default (must include notice of right to mediation) and a 3 week notice of sale.
Time to Respond	N/A (responding to mediation availability is wise)
Loan Reinstatement Options	Available within 35 days of default
Loan Redemption Options	N/A
Deficiency Judgments	Generally not allowed
Eviction Procedure	Must give 3 day written notice to leave and then file for court order to evict
Foreclosure Statutes	Nev. Rev. Stat. § 107.080

New Hampshire	
General foreclosure type	Non-Judicial
Estimated Process Period When Uncontested	45-60 days
Sale Publish Period	2 options: Personal service at least 25 days prior to sale or publishing for 3 consecutive weeks
Time to Respond	N/A
Loan Reinstatement Options	N/A
Loan Redemption Options	N/A
Deficiency Judgments	Generally able to obtain by filing a separate suit
Eviction Procedure	Must give 30 day written notice to leave and then obtain a court order for eviction
Foreclosure Statutes	N.H. Rev. Stat. Ann. § 479:25

New Jersey	
General foreclosure type	Judicial
Estimated Process Period When Uncontested	180-300 days
Sale Publish Period	Must send certified mail notice to homeowner 30 days before filing a foreclosure lawsuit. Foreclosing party must also post notice on the property 4 times in 4 weeks before filing suit.
Time to Respond	20-30 days
Loan Reinstatement Options	Available up to date of final judgment. Court may delay judgment if homeowner needs extra time to reinstate.
Loan Redemption Options	Generally N/A; 6 months if deficiency judgment is obtained
Deficiency Judgments	Limited deficiencies allowed by filing a separate suit within 3 months of sale
Eviction Procedure	Automatic with sale
Foreclosure Statutes	N.J. Stat. Ann. §§ 2A:50-1 to 2A:50-21, 2A:50-56 to 2A:50-58

New Mexico	
General foreclosure type	Both
Estimated Process Period When Uncontested	120-180 days
Sale Publish Period	Judicial: After judgment issued, sale may not occur for 30 days. Must publish notice of sale for 4 consecutive weeks before sale and also post notices in 6 of the most public places in the county. Non-judicial: 90 days after notice of sale is completed
Time to Respond	Judicial: 20-30 days depending on service Non-Judicial: N/A
Loan Reinstatement Options	Judicial: 30-day opportunity to reinstate before filing of complaint or any time prior to foreclosure sale Non-judicial: N/A
Loan Redemption Options	Judicial: Available after judgment and before sale. Available for nine months after sale (must pay 10% penalty) Non-judicial: Available for nine months after sale
Deficiency Judgments	Judicial: Allowed Non-Judicial: Must file separate suit
Eviction Procedure	Must give 3 day written notice to leave and then file for court order of eviction
Foreclosure Statutes	N.M. Stat. Ann. §§ 48-7-1 to 48-7-24, 39-5-1 to 39-5-23 (judicial); 48-10-1 to 48-10-21 (non-judicial)

New York	
General foreclosure type	Judicial
Estimated Process Period When Uncontested	1 year
Sale Publish Period	Must provide advisory to homeowner at least 90 days before filing foreclosure complaint. If foreclosure judgment is granted, notice of sale must be served by publication.
Time to Respond	20-30 days depending on service type
Loan Reinstatement Options	Available any time before final foreclosure judgment and any time before sale
Loan Redemption Options	N/A
Deficiency Judgments	Allowed (only if homeowner is personally served or appears in court)
Eviction Procedure	Must provide 10 day written notice to leave and then get a court order for eviction
Foreclosure Statutes	N.Y. Real Prop. Acts. Law §§ 1301 to 1391

North Carolina	
General foreclosure type	Both; non-judicial favored (property can't be sold until the court holds a hearing, reviews the paperwork, and certifies sale)
Estimated Process Period When Uncontested	105-120 days
Sale Publish Period	Notice about housing counselors required prior to filing notice of default. Notice of default must be filed 30 days before notice of hearing. Notice of hearing must be given 10 days before the hearing. If foreclosure approved at hearing, homeowner must be served with a 10-20 day notice, depending upon service type.
Time to Respond	N/A
Loan Reinstatement Options	N/A
Loan Redemption Options	Available for 10 days after sale
Deficiency Judgments	Generally N/A
Eviction Procedure	Must provide 10 day written notice to leave and then get a court order for eviction
Foreclosure Statutes	N.C. Gen. Stat. §§ 45-21.1 to 45-21.33, 45-100 to 47-107

North Dakota	
General foreclosure type	Judicial
Estimated Process Period When Uncontested	120-180 days
Sale Publish Period	Must serve homeowner with notice of intent to foreclose 30-90 days prior to filing complaint. Notice of sale must be published or posted on courthouse door and five other places.
Time to Respond	20-30 days depending on service type
Loan Reinstatement Options	Available for 30 days after notice of intent to foreclose
Loan Redemption Options	Available for 60 days after sale
Deficiency Judgments	N/A
Eviction Procedure	Automatic after redemption period ends
Foreclosure Statutes	N.D. Cent. Code §§ 32-19-01 to 32-19-41

Ohio	
General foreclosure type	Judicial
Estimated Process Period When Uncontested	180-240 days
Sale Publish Period	After judgment is issued, must file notice of sale with the court at least 7 days prior to the sale and send homeowner a copy by mail. Must also publish for 3 weeks prior to sale.
Time to Respond	28 days
Loan Reinstatement Options	N/A
Loan Redemption Options	Available until court confirms sale
Deficiency Judgments	Allowed, but void after 2 years and must meet specific criteria for amount
Eviction Procedure	Not specifically outlined in statute so likely need to obtain a court order for eviction
Foreclosure Statutes	Ohio Rev. Code Ann. §§ 2323.07, 2329.26, 5721.38

Oklahoma	
General foreclosure type	Both; judicial favored
Estimated Process Period When Uncontested	150-210 days
Sale Publish Period	After judgment is issued, lender must serve a notice of sale on homeowner by mail and publish notice of sale at least 30 days before the sale.
Time to Respond	20-30 days depending on service type
Loan Reinstatement Options	N/A
Loan Redemption Options	Allowed until court confirms sale
Deficiency Judgments	Allowed within 90 days of sale but limited by market value
Eviction Procedure	Immediate possession to new owner
Foreclosure Statutes	Okla. Stat. tit. 12, §§ 686, 764 to 765, 773; Okla. Stat. tit. 46, §§ 41 to 49

Oregon	
General foreclosure type	Both; non-judicial favored
Estimated Process Period When Uncontested	150-180 days
Sale Publish Period	Must record a notice of default and serve it on homeowner. Must also serve a notice of sale on homeowner 120 days prior to sale.
Time to Respond	N/A
Loan Reinstatement Options	Available until 5 days prior to sale
Loan Redemption Options	N/A
Deficiency Judgments	N/A
Eviction Procedure	Automatic 10 days after sale
Foreclosure Statutes	Or. Rev. Stat. §§ 86.735 to 86.795, 88.080 to 88.100

Pennsylvania	
General foreclosure type	Judicial
Estimated Process Period When Uncontested	240-300 days
Sale Publish Period	Before filing a complaint in court, the foreclosing party must serve a 30-day notice of intention to foreclose on homeowner by certified mail.
Time to Respond	20-30 days depending on service type
Loan Reinstatement Options	Available until sale
Loan Redemption Options	N/A
Deficiency Judgments	Allowed, but must file separate suit
Eviction Procedure	Not specifically outlined in statute so likely need to obtain a court order for eviction
Foreclosure Statutes	Pa. Stat. Ann. tit. 35, §§ 1680.402c to 1680.409c; Pa. Stat. Ann. tit. 41, §§ 403 to 404; Pa. R. Civ. P. 1141-1150

Rhode Island	
General foreclosure type	Non-Judicial
Estimated Process Period When Uncontested	75-90 days
Sale Publish Period	Must serve homeowner with a foreclosure counseling notice at least 45 days before foreclosure is initiated. Notice of sale must be certified mailed to homeowner at least 30 days before publishing and then published for 3 consecutive weeks before sale with all 3 occurring between 21 and 7 days prior to sale.
Time to Respond	N/A
Loan Reinstatement Options	N/A
Loan Redemption Options	Available up to 3 years after sale but former owner must file suit to redeem
Deficiency Judgments	Allowed, but must file separate suit
Eviction Procedure	Must file complaint for eviction; former owner has 20 days to respond
Foreclosure Statutes	R.I. Gen. Laws §§ 34-27-1 to 34-27-5

South Carolina	
General foreclosure type	Judicial
Estimated Process Period When Uncontested	150 days
Sale Publish Period	After judgment is issued, must publish notice of sale and also post it in 3 public places at least 3 weeks prior to sale.
Time to Respond	20-30 days depending on service type
Loan Reinstatement Options	N/A
Loan Redemption Options	N/A
Deficiency Judgments	Allowed
Eviction Procedure	10 day written notice
Foreclosure Statutes	S.C. Code Ann. §§ 15-39-610, 29-3-630 to 29-3-790

	South Dakota
General foreclosure type	Both; non-judicial is favored but homeowners may choose judicial
Estimated Process Period When Uncontested	90-180 days
Sale Publish Period	Before foreclosure, must publish notice once a week for 4 weeks and must serve homeowner with written notice 21 days before sale (notice explains how to elect judicial foreclosure)
Time to Respond	Must elect to have judicial foreclosure and then have 20-30 days once served
Loan Reinstatement Options	Judicial: Available until judgment is entered Non-Judicial: N/A
Loan Redemption Options	Judicial: 1 year (sometimes conditions in the mortgage allow for only 6 months) Non-judicial: N/A
Deficiency Judgments	Allowed, but may be limited
Eviction Procedure	Judicial: After redemption period ends, new owner must give occupant a 3 day notice to leave and then obtain an eviction order. Non-judicial: Not specifically outlined in statute so likely need to obtain a court order for eviction
Foreclosure Statutes	S.D. Cod. Laws Ann. §§ 21-48-1 to 21-48-26

Tennessee	
General foreclosure type	Non-Judicial
Estimated Process Period When Uncontested	45-60 days
Sale Publish Period	Must send by registered mail a notice of right to foreclose on or before the first publication of the notice of sale. Must then either publish notice of sale 20 days before sale or post notice on property 30 days before sale.
Time to Respond	N/A
Loan Reinstatement Options	N/A
Loan Redemption Options	2 years (may be waived in mortgage documentation though)
Deficiency Judgments	Allowed, but must file separate suit and may be limited in amount
Eviction Procedure	Must obtain court order
Foreclosure Statutes	Tenn. Code Ann. §§ 35-5-101 to 35-5-111, 66-8-101 to 66-8-102

Texas	
General foreclosure type	Both; non-judicial favored
Estimated Process Period When Uncontested	45 days
Sale Publish Period	Must serve notice of default 20 days before serving notice of sale. Notice of sale must be served by mail on homeowner 21 days before sale and posted on courthouse door.
Time to Respond	N/A
Loan Reinstatement Options	Available until 20 days after receiving notice of default
Loan Redemption Options	N/A
Deficiency Judgments	Allowed; must file separate suit within 2 years (may be limited in amount)
Eviction Procedure	3 day written notice and then must obtain a court order to evict
Foreclosure Statutes	Tex. Prop. Code Ann. § 51.002

Utah	
General foreclosure type	Non-Judicial
Estimated Process Period When Uncontested	120-150 days
Sale Publish Period	Must record notice of default at least 3 months prior to sale and mail homeowner a copy. After 3 months, must publish a notice of sale 3 times; the last date of publication must be 10-30 days before the sale. Notice of sale must also be posted on property at least 20 days prior sale.
Time to Respond	N/A
Loan Reinstatement Options	Allowed for 3 months after notice of default is recorded
Loan Redemption Options	N/A
Deficiency Judgments	Allowed; must file separate suit within 2 years (limited in amount)
Eviction Procedure	5 day written notice and then must obtain a court order to evict
Foreclosure Statutes	Utah Code Ann. §§ 57-1-19, 78B-6-901

Vermont	
General foreclosure type	Judicial
Estimated Process Period When Uncontested	90-120 days
Sale Publish Period	N/A (strict foreclosure)
Time to Respond	20-30 days depending on service type
Loan Reinstatement Options	Available upon agreement prior to sale
Loan Redemption Options	6 months (may be altered by court order or mutual agreement)
Deficiency Judgments	Allowed, but must be requested in the foreclosure complaint and is limited in amount.
Eviction Procedure	After redemption period expires, new owner must serve a writ of eviction on occupants who then have 30 days to vacate.
Foreclosure Statutes	Vt. Stat. Ann. tit. 12, §§ 4526-4533a

Virginia	
General foreclosure type	Non-Judicial
Estimated Process Period When Uncontested	60 days
Sale Publish Period	Foreclosing party must serve notice of sale on homeowner by mail or publication (time frame unspecified). Mail is usually used as publication rules are highly complicated.
Time to Respond	14 days
Loan Reinstatement Options	N/A
Loan Redemption Options	N/A
Deficiency Judgments	Allowed, must file separate suit
Eviction Procedure	Must obtain court order
Foreclosure Statutes	Va. Code Ann. §§ 55-59 to 55-66.6

Washington	
General foreclosure type	Both; non-judicial favored
Estimated Process Period When Uncontested	210 days
Sale Publish Period	Must contact homeowner at least 30 days before issuing a notice of default for owner-occupied residential properties to try to reach an amicable resolution (response = no default can be filed for 60 days). A notice of default must be served on homeowner 30 days before notice of sale by certified mail and posting on the property or by personal service. Must serve notice of sale in the same manner as the notice of default at least 90 days before sale date. No sale may occur within 190 days after the first default.
Time to Respond	30 days (prior to notice of default)
Loan Reinstatement Options	Available up to 11 days before sale
Loan Redemption Options	Non-Judicial: N/A Judicial: 8-12 months, depending on circumstances
Deficiency Judgments	Only available for judicial foreclosures
Eviction Procedure	Automatic after 20 days from sale
Foreclosure Statutes	Wash. Rev. Code §§ 61.24.020 to 61.24.140

Washington, D.C.	
General foreclosure type	Non-Judicial
Estimated Process Period When Uncontested	60-105 days
Sale Publish Period	Default notice must be served by certified mail on homeowner and mayor. Must file Notice of Sale at least 30 days prior to sale. Sale may be postponed up to 60 additional days to allow for mediation.
Time to Respond	N/A
Loan Reinstatement Options	Available up to 5 days before sale
Loan Redemption Options	N/A
Deficiency Judgments	May be obtained by filing a lawsuit
Eviction Procedure	Must file suit and give at least 7 days' notice prior to the hearing for eviction
Foreclosure Statutes	D.C. Code Ann. §§ 42-815, 42-816

West Virginia	
General foreclosure type	Non-Judicial
Estimated Process Period When Uncontested	60-90 days
Sale Publish Period	Must provide notice within a reasonable time before sale by publishing notice and by sending it through registered mail.
Time to Respond	N/A
Loan Reinstatement Options	Available for 10 days after served with notice of right to cure, which can be served 5 days after default
Loan Redemption Options	N/A
Deficiency Judgments	Allowed
Eviction Procedure	Not specifically outlined in statute so likely need to obtain a court order for eviction
Foreclosure Statutes	W. Va. Code §§ 38-1-3 to 38-1-15

Wisconsin	
General foreclosure type	Judicial
Estimated Process Period When Uncontested	1 year or more
Sale Publish Period	Sale must be at least 1 year after the judgment is entered (6 months if the foreclosing party waives its right to a deficiency). Notice of sale must either be published over a 6 week period or posted over a 3 week period.
Time to Respond	20-30 days depending on service type
Loan Reinstatement Options	Available any time before judgment
Loan Redemption Options	N/A post sale. Can be redeemed prior to sale (after judgment) – time period ranges from 5 weeks to 1 year
Deficiency Judgments	Must be requested in foreclosure complaint
Eviction Procedure	Confirmation of the sale will usually entitle the plaintiff to a writ of eviction
Foreclosure Statutes	Wis. Stat. §§ 846.01 to 846.25

Wyoming	
General foreclosure type	Both; non-judicial favored
Estimated Process Period When Uncontested	60 days
Sale Publish Period	Must serve notice of intent to foreclose on homeowner 10 days before first publication of the notice of sale. Notice of sale must be published for 4 weeks before sale and served on homeowner before date of first publication.
Time to Respond	N/A
Loan Reinstatement Options	N/A
Loan Redemption Options	3 months
Deficiency Judgments	Allowed
Eviction Procedure	Not specifically outlined in statute so likely need to obtain a court order for eviction
Foreclosure Statutes	Judicial: Wyo. Stat. Ann. §§ 1-18-101 to 1-18-114 Non-judicial: Wyo. Stat. Ann. §§ 34-4-101 to 34-4-113

Appendix B: Listing of common loan servicers' contact information

Mortgage Servicer	Fax No. for Letter of Authorization	Borrower Follow-up Phone Number
American Home Mtg	866-795-6529 866-809-6900	877-304-3100
Americas Servicing Co.	866-453-6315 866-590-8910	800-662-3806
Aurora Loan Service	303-728-7648	800-550-0508
Bank of America	805-520-5019	800-846-2222
B B & T	252-293-9058	800-827-3722 800-790-9502
Carrington Mtg Svcs	949-517-5170	800-827-3722
Chase Bank	888-249-1593	877-838-1882
Chevy Chase Bank (Sold to Capital One)	301-939-4988	800-933-9100
Citimortgage	480-753-7832	800-283-7918
Colonial Savings	817-390-2345	800-937-6303
Countrywide	805-520-5019	877-744-7691
EMC	214-626-4704	866-325-4314
Everhome Mortgage	904-281-6380	800-669-7724
First Horizon	214-441-5794	800-489-2966
GMAC Homecomings	866-501-1610	800-850-4622
Greentree		877-816-9125
HFC (handles HSBC)	732-352-7519	800-333-5848
Homeq Servicing	866-554-5325	877-867-7378
HSBC	888-629-8590	888-648-3124
IndyMac Bank	269-353-2474	877-736-5556

JPMorgan Chase	866-931-9938	800-848-9136
Litton Loan Servicing	713-314-4705	800-548-8665
Met Life Home Loans	214-441-4594	800-364-7662
Midland Mortgage	260-459-5390	800-552-3000
National City Mtg Co	937-910-3333	800-283-7918 800-622-5035
Nationstar Mtg LLC	972-315-6827	888-850-9398
Ocwen Mortgage Corp	407-737-5693	877-596-8580
Option One (changed to American Home Mtg svc)	949-790-8505	877-304-3100
Regions Bank	601-554-2385	800-748-9498
RBC	866-661-0782	877-252-8226
Saxon Mortgage	817-665-7970	888-325-3502
SunTrust Mortgage	804-745-8115	800-443-1082
U.S. Bank	904-268-7179	888-780-3997
Wachovia	210-509-1174	866-587-4014
Washington Mutual	843-673-3509 800-225-5497	888-926-8937
Wells Fargo	866-917-1877	877-216-8448

Appendix C: List of Known Robosigners

- Aimee Austin
- Amie Davis
- Amy Jo Cauthern-Munoz
- Amy Payment
- Amy Weis
- Andrew Keardy
- Angela L. Freckman
- Andres Rojas
- Ann Pinto
- Anne Sutcliffe
- Annmarie Morrison
- Azin Rahmanpanah
- Bernadette Polux
- Bernice Thell
- Beverly Clark
- Bharati Lengade
- Brian J. LaForest
- Brock Martin
- Cardless Dixon
- Carolyn Mcleod
- Cathy Hagstrom
- Charmaine Marchesi
- Christopher Bray
- Chyrs Houston
- Clifton Childs
- Craig Hanlon
- Craig Hinson
- Dawn L. Reynolds
- Denise A. Marvel
- Donna McNaught
- Dory Goebel
- Dulce Diaz
- Eileen J. Gonzales
- Elizabeth Geretschlaeger
- Emmanuel Tabot
- Erika Reyes
- Erika Spencer
- Etsuko Kaybeya
- Fanessa Fuller
- Fedelis Fondunggallah
- Felix Amenumey
- Fifi Volgarkis
- Frank Coon
- Gloria Karau
- Hang Luu
- Hari Charagundla
- Indgrid Pittman
- Jacqueline Brown
- Jamie Bilot
- Jamil Kahin
- Jan Zimmerman
- Janeete Boatman
- Janice M. Baker
- Jason Dreher
- Jason Emory
- Jeff Rivas
- Jennifer Duncan
- Jeremy Cox
- Jerrie Moton
- Jerry Yang
- Joel Martinson
- John Cody
- Joseph Alvarado

- Joseph Lutz
- Joseph P. Hillery
- Judith Stone
- Julie Coon
- Katie Zrust
- Katrina Bailey
- Katrina Whitfield
- Keith Chapman
- Keith S. Reno
- Kevin Fletcher
- Keo Maney
- Kue Vang
- Kim Kenny
- Kim Kinney
- Kim Mullins
- Kim Waldroff
- Kimberly Sanford
- Kimley Godfrey
- Kimbretta Duncan
- Kyurstina Lawton
- Larry Dingmann
- Laura Hescott
- Leticia Arias
- Lindsay Lesch
- Lisa Gerard
- Marcia Medley
- Margie Kwiatanowsk
- Marisa G. Carrasco
- Margery A. Rotundo
- Marisa Menza
- Martha Kunkle
- Maya Stevenson
- Mellisa Ziertman
- Mellissa Mosloski
- Melody Moore
- Michael Ackerman
- Michael H. Moreland
- Michael Hanna
- Michele Boiko
- Michelle Flores
- Michelle Halyard
- Mutru Kumar
- Natalie Anderson
- Neil E. Dyson
- Paige Sahr
- Pam Anderson
- Pam Kammerer
- Pam January
- Pat Kingston
- Paul Bruha
- Paul Hunt
- Paul Mann
- Peggy Glass
- Peter Read
- R.P. Umali
- Rashonda Turner
- Rebecca Verdeja
- Renae Stanton
- Renee L. Hensley
- Richard Delgado
- Richard Olasande
- Rick Wilken
- Robert E. Kaltenbach
- Robyn Colburn
- Rodney Cadwell
- Rona Ramos
- Roy Stringfellow
- Sakhada Lad
- Salena Edwards
- Sara Rubin
- Sarah Block
- Sarah Rubin
- Scott Anderson
- Scott Keller
- Scott W. Anderson
- September Stoudemire

- Sheri Bongaarts
- Shivani L. Ram
- Silvia Marchan
- Stanley Silva
- Steve A. Nielsen
- Steve Ballman
- Steve Moe
- Steven Grount
- Sue Fillczkowski
- Susan Nightingale
- Tam Doan
- Tammy Brooks-Saleh
- Tammy Saleh
- Taylor Moore
- Teresa DeBaker
- Tina Jones
- Tishana Gibbs
- Toccoa Lenair
- Treva Moreland
- Van Johnson
- Varsha Thakkar
- Verdine A Freeman
- Vicki Kyle
- Victor Perez
- Vinod Vishwakarma
- Vishal Karingada
- Whitney Lewis
- Yvette Day

Appendix D: Listing of Major Foreclosure Mills by State

- **Alaska:**
  Alaska Trustee, LLC
  AK,HI,ID,MT,OR,WA,TX Malcolm Cisneros
  AK,HI,ID,MT,OR,WA,TX Trustee Corps.
  Regional Trustee Services
- **Alabama:**
  SIROTE & PERMUTT, P.C.
  AL/MS Dumas and McPhail, L.L.C.
  Shapiro & Pickett, LLP
  Scott J. Humphrey
  Albertelli Law
- **Arkansas:**
  Mickel Law Firm, PA
  Robert S. Coleman, Jr., P.A.
  Wilson & Associates, PLLC
  Dyke, Henry, Goldsholl
  Baxter and Schwartz PC
- **Arizona:**
  Malcolm & Cisneros
  Tiffany & Bosco
  Statewide Foreclosure Services
  Folks & O'Connor, PLLC
  AZ/NV/OR/UT/WA Law Offices of Les Zieve
- **California:**
  Old Republic Default Management Services
  Solomon Grindle Silverman & Spinella
  Malcolm & Cisneros
  Curtis Law Group
  Housekey

Quality Loan Service Corp
OPTION ONE
Fremont Investment and Loan Management
Aztec Foreclosure Corp
Old Republic Default Management Services

- **Colorado:**
  Aronowitz & Ford, LLP
  Robert J. Hopp & Associates, LLC
  Edwards & Taylor, LLC
  Frascona, Joiner, Goodman and Greenstein
  Janeway Law Firm, PC
  Moss Codilis
  Castle, Meinhold & Stawiarski
  Hellerstine & Shore

- **Connecticut:**
  Reiner, Reiner & Bendett
  HUNT LIEBERT
  CT/DC/MD/VA McCabe, Weisberg and Conway
  Law Office of Martha Croog

- **Washington, D.C.:**
  Rosenberg & Associates, LLC
  MD/DC/VA Bierman, Geesing & Ward, LLC
  CT/DC/ McCabe, Weisberg and Conway
  DC/VA Curran & O'Sullivan, PC

- **Delaware:**
  Draper & Goldberg
  Whittington & Aulgur
  Young Conaway Stargatt & Taylor

- **Florida:**
  HOLLAND & KNIGHT
  Jonathan Kilne, PA
  FL/PA Joseph H Ganguzza & Associates
  David J. Stern, PA
  Marshall C. Watson
  Gary I. Gassel, PA
  Law Offices of Daniel C. Consuegra

Ben Ezra Law Firm
Phillips, Flynn, Dareneau
Shapiro & Fishman
Smith, Hiatt & Diaz
Albertelli & Halsema
Enrico Gonzales
Popkin & Rosaler

- **Georgia:**
  Ellis, Painter, Ratterree & Adams
  McCalla, Raymer, Padrick, Cobb, Nichols & Clark
  Shapiro & Swertfeger
  McCurdy & Candler, L.L.C.
  Stites & Harbison
  Richard B. Maner
  Stephen J. Knezo
  Albertelli & Halsema, PL
  Flanagan & Ireland
  Moore & Associates
  Shuping, Morse & Ross
  MORRIS, SCHNEIDER, PRIOR, JOHNSON & FREEDMAN, LLC

- **Hawaii:**
  AK,HI,ID,MT,OR,WA,TX Malcolm Cisneros
  AK,HI,ID,MT,OR,WA,TX Trustee Corps.
  Pite, Duncan & Melmet

- **Idaho:**
  AK,HI,ID,MT,OR,WA,TX Malcolm Cisneros
  AK,HI,ID,MT,OR,WA,TX Trustee Corps.
  McCarthy & Holthus
  Regional Trustee Services
  Alliance Default Services

- **Illinois:**
  Kluever and Platt
  Dutton & Dutton
  Jaros, Tittle & O'Toole
  IL/MI/OH/PA Weltman, Weinberg and Reis
  Codilis & Associates

Wirbicki Law Group
Heavner, Scott, Beyers & Mihlar
Fisher & Shapiro
Freedman, Anselmo, Lindberg & Rappe

- **Indiana:**
  Bleecker Brodey and Andrews
  KY/IN/OH Reisenfeld & Associates
  Nelson & Frankenberger
  Feiwell & Hannoy
  Foutty & Foutty
  Doyle and Friedmeyer

- **Iowa:**
  Belin, Harris, Lamson & McCormic
  Dunakey & Klatt
  Petosa, Petosa & Boecker

- **Kansas:**
  Kozeny & McCubbin
  Martin, Leigh, Laws & Fritzlen
  Shapiro & Mock
  Shapiro & Reid
  South & Associates
  Gallas & Schultz

- **Kentucky:**
  KY/IN Reisenfeld & Associates
  Manley Deas Kochalski, LLC
  Reynolds & Thompson, LLP
  Nielson & Sherry
  Lerner, Sampson & Rothfuss
  Clunk, Paisley and Assoc., PSC
  Mapother & Mapother

- **Louisiana:**
  The Boles Law Firm
  Foreclosure Law Firm, LLC
  Shapiro & Mentz
  Dean Morris

- **Massachusetts:**
  Korde & Associates
  Ablitt & Charlton
  DOONAN, GRAVES & LONGORIA
  MA/NH/RI Orlans Moran PLLC

- **Maryland:**
  The Fisher Law Group, PLLC
  CT/DC/MD/VA McCabe, Weisberg and Conway
  MD/DC/VA Bierman, Geesing & Ward, LLC
  Friedman & MacFadyen, PA
  Cohn, Goldberg & Deutsch
  Shapiro & Burson
  Rosenberg and Associates

- **Maine:**
  Shapiro & Morley, LLP

- **Michigan:**
  Potestivo & Associates
  Trott & Trott (also listed as MN)
  IL/MI/OH/PA Weltman, Weinberg and Reis
  Orlans Associates
  Fabrizio & Brook
  Peter, Schneiderman & Associates

- **Minnesota:**
  TROTT AND TROTT, P.C.
  Usset & Weingarden, PLLP
  Shapiro, Nordmeyer & Zielke, LLP.
  Elizabeth Mason, PC
  Murnane Brandt

- **Missouri:**
  Codilis, Stawiarski & Moody
  Martin, Leigh, Laws & Fritzlen
  Kozeny & McCubbin
  Millsap & Singer
  Sandberg, Phoenix and Von Gontart
  South & Associates

- **Mississippi:**
  Adams & Edens PA
  Shapiro & Massey
  Dyke, Henry, Goldsholl
  AL/MS Dumas and McPhail, L.L.C.
  Morris and Associates (a/k/a Morris Law Firm)
  Morris, Schneider & Prior, LLC

- **Montana:**
  AK,HI,ID,MT,OR,WA,TX Malcolm Cisneros
  AK,HI,ID,MT,OR,WA,TX Trustee Corps.
  Just Law Office
  Mackoff, Kellogg, Kirby & Klos

- **North Carolina:**
  Shapiro & Ingle
  Morris, Schneider & Prior, LLC
  Brock & Scott
  Nodell, Glass & Haskell
  Roberson, Haworth & Reese
  Erwin, Simpson & Stroud

- **Nebraska:**
  Kozeny & McCubbin
  Eric H. Linquist

- **New Hampshire:**
  Harmon Law Offices, PC
  Korde & Associates
  Barron & Stadfeld, PC
  Shechtman Halperin Savage, LLP
  MA/NH/RI Orlans Moran PLLC
  NH/VT Law Offices of Jonathan F. Weidman

- **New Jersey:**
  Fein, Such, Kahn & Shepard
  Zucker, Goldberg & Ackerman
  Koury, Tighe, Lapres, Bisulca & Sommers
  PLUESE, BECKER & SALTZMAN
  McCabe Weisberg

NJ/PA Stern & Eisenberg, LLP
Parker McCay

- **New Mexico:**
  Little & Dranttel
- **Nevada:**
  Malcolm & Cisneros
  Aztec Foreclosure Corp
  McCarthy & Holthus
  National Default Servicing Corp.
  AZ/NV/OR/UT/WA Law Offices of Les Zieve
- **New York:**
  Jonathan D. Pincus
  Shapiro & DiCaro
  McCabe Weisberg
  Rosicki, Rosicki & Associates
  Ziccardi & Rella PC
  Edward A/ Wiener, Esq.
  Eschen, Frenkel & Weisman
  Cohn & Roth
  Steven J. Baum
  Berkman Henoch Peterson & Peddy, PC
- **Ohio:**
  IL/MI/OH/PA Weltman, Weinberg and Reis
  Shapiro & Felty
  Manley Deas & Kochalski
  KY/IN/OH Reisenfeld & Associates
  LERNER, SAMPSON & ROTHFUSS
  LAURITO & LAURITO
  Luper, Neidenthal and Logan
  Law Offices of John D. Clunk Co., LPA
  Keith D. Wiener & Assoc.
  Reimer, Lorber & Arnovitz Co.
  Carlisle McNellie Law Firm
  Gerner & Kearns Co., LPA
- **Oklahoma:**
  BAER, TIMBERLAKE, COULSON & CATES

Lamun, Mock, Cunnyngham & Davis
Shapiro & Cejda
Kivell, Rayment and Francis

- **Oregon:**
  Shapiro & Sutherland, LLC
  OR/WA Bishop White & Marshal
  AK,HI,ID,MT,OR,WA,TX Malcolm Cisneros
  AK,HI,ID,MT,OR,WA,TX Trustee Corps.
  Robinson Tait
  Routh Crabtree Olsen
  AZ/NV/OR/UT/WA Law Offices of Les Zieve

- **Pennsylvania:**
  Shapiro & Kreisman
  FL/PA Joseph H Ganguzza & Associates
  Goldbeck McCafferty & McKeever
  McCabe Weisberg (McCabe, Weisberg, Conway)
  Shaffer & Scerni
  Udren Law Offices
  Zucker, Goldberg, Ackerman
  Martha Von Rosenstiel
  IL/MI/OH/PA Weltman, Weinberg and Reis
  NJ/PA Stern & Eisenberg, LLP
  Law Offices of Barbara A. Fein

- **Rhode Island:**
  Nicholas Barrett & Assoc.
  MA/NH/RI Orlans Moran PLLC

- **South Carolina:**
  Finkel Law Firm, LLC
  Roger, Townsend, and Thomas
  Weston Adams Law Firm
  McDonald McKenzie
  SC, TN Brock & Scott, PLLC
  Fleming and Whitt, P.A.
  Riley Pope & Laney
  Bolen Law Firm

- **South Dakota:**
  Mackoff, Kellogg, Kirby & Klos
- **Tennessee:**
  Shapiro & Kirsch
  Apperson, Crump, Duzane & Maxwell PLC
  SC, TN Brock & Scott, PLLC
  Richard B. Maner, PC
  Rodgers, Hill and Kolarich
  McCurdy & Candler
  Wilson & Associates
- **Texas:**
  Winstead Sechrest & Minick P.C.
  Hughes Watters Askanase
  AK,HI,ID,MT,OR,WA,TX Trustee Corps.
  Robertson & Anschutz, P.C.
  Barrett Burke Wilson Castle Daffin & Frappier
  Baxter & Schwartz
  Brice, Vander Linden & Wernick
  Brown & Shapiro
  Codilis & Stawiarski
  Mann & Stevens
  Kelly Harvey
  AK,HI,ID,MT,OR,WA,TX Malcolm Cisneros
- **Utah:**
  SCALLEY READING BATES HANSEN & RASMUSSEN, P.C.
  CMS Legal Services
  David B. Boyce
  Scalley, Reading, Bates, Hansen & Rasmussen
  AZ/NV/OR/UT/WA Law Offices of Les Zieve
- **Virginia:**
  Shapiro & Burson
  Friedman and MacFadyen
  Sykes, Bourdon, Ahern & Levy
  Samuel I. White P.C.
  Specialized, Inc. of Virginia
  Rosenberg & Associates, LLC
  Glasser and Glasser, P.L.C.

MD/DC/VA Bierman, Geesing & Ward, LLC
CT/DC/ MD/VA McCabe, Weisberg and Conway
DC/VA Curran & O'Sullivan, PC

- **Vermont:**
  Lobe & Fortin
  NH/VT Law Offices of Jonathan F. Weidman
  Jeffery Kosterich & Associates, PC
- **Washington:**
  Robinson Tait
  AK,HI,ID,MT,OR,WA,TX Malcolm Cisneros
  AK,HI,ID,MT,OR,WA,TX Trustee Corps.
  OR/WA Bishop White & Marshal
  Meridian Trust Deed Service
  Quality Loan Service Corp.
  Routh Crabtree Olsen
  Shapiro & Sutherland
  AZ/NV/OR/UT/WA Law Offices of Les Zieve
- **West Virginia:**
  Law Office of D. Kevin Moffatt
  Daniel J. Mancini and Associates
- **Wisconsin:**
  Vollmar and Huismann, S.C.
  GRAY & ASSOCIATES
  Blommer Peterman
- **Wyoming:**
  Castle, Meinhold & Stawiarski

Appendix E: Sample Case Studies

Over the past few years I've witnessed some astounding tales involving families and their homes – some fantastic, others horrifying. A few were just shocking, even humorous. It's always difficult to bear the tragic accounts, even more so when it could have been prevented. Conversely, I thoroughly enjoy seeing families rise from surviving to thriving. I've decided to disclose a few of these anecdotes to show with real-world examples the varying topics that have been discussed throughout this book. Pay particular attention to the unique lessons contained within each. We'll start with the case I know best – my father's.

Case Study #1: Glenn Prentice is a middle-aged father of five. He had been highly successful in his life, rising from a poverty-stricken youth to seven figure net worth and six figure income by his late twenties. This was achieved by growing a business from the ground up, while carefully managing his money. Through divorce, his finances took a steep pitfall. However, Glenn quickly recovered and by his mid-thirties was yet again on track for early retirement.

Life was comfortable for my father. Then he got in a bad car accident, resulting in brain injury and spinal damage. Several complications later, it was determined that he would never recover fully. Shortly thereafter, his second wife collapsed – her heartbeat ceased for 29 minutes before being revived. She survived, but due to lack of oxygen to the brain, would never again be a fully functioning adult. Tragic, unforeseeable incidents led to incredible medical bills. Glenn's business was sold to cover some of these. Within months he went from on top of the world financially to millions of dollars in debt, with insufficient physical capability to work.

Why do I point all of this personal, seemingly irrelevant information out? Because it's not irrelevant at all. A significant percentage of those facing foreclosure got in that position not because they were overextended, but because they encountered extreme hardship. Medical problems, deaths, job losses – all reasons why some became unable to make ends meet.

My dad's home was underwater when he received his foreclosure notice, but not by much. His problem wasn't equity, it was income – he didn't have any. This is a common affliction of those facing foreclosures. As you know from reading this far, my general advice now would be "Don't try to keep it". This isn't always an option for those with minor children. Going against his principals (my dad had never missed a house payment in his life), Glenn did what he had to do to survive – he contested foreclosure with the intent of keeping his home or at least delaying the foreclosure as long as possible.

Mr. Prentice was highly successful at achieving this goal – 5 years without a payment is quite a feat in a non-judicial state, especially without an attorney or any legal guidance. I'm proud of my father. He did something that's tough for most; he swallowed his pride. I've advised many people that the best path for their family is utilizing the legal system to buy time. Some have been grateful for the honest advice, others have shunned it. Guiding someone on their morals is not something I'm willing to do; that's an internal journey.

Not every filing with the sole objective of obtaining time works out so well, but for Glenn it certainly did. He used that time as it should be used – to increase his means and save money. Taking it a step further, Glenn also used his experience to teach others. These days the foreclosure is behind him, he's settled in a new home, and his health is improving. Perhaps his example will show others that the clichéd "fresh start" is possible.

Moving on to some less personal examples, I've highlighted 15 varying circumstances, what they resulted in, and what lesson that can impart. For privacy reasons, all names have been altered. The facts of each case remain intact.

Case Study #2: Mr. White came to me after he had already been through a poor experience with a prior law office. His case was well underway and was a complete mess. He was fighting in multiple courts and his matter was further complicated with a bankruptcy. The intricacies of the case are too vast for our purposes here. Suffice to say, he had some decent core arguments, but more importantly a very reasonable objective. Mr. White was fortunate to have some affluent friends that were willing to pay a one-time sum on his behalf should the bank be willing to settle the case. His note was for approximately $200,000 and the home was worth less than half of that at the time. Despite having a meritorious case already in federal court, this client decided to offer his lender a settlement: He would pay $150,000 in a cashier's check within 30 days to completely satisfy the note. This offer was flatly denied. No counter, no discussion; a simple "No.". This case is still active today with no end in sight. My point: Never assume any resolution is open and shut, no matter how reasonable.

Case Study #3: Mr. Blue had a predicament. He had fallen behind on his mortgage for a length of time because he had been going through a rough divorce. Once the foreclosure came, he was faced with a conundrum. His loan was accelerated and while he had some money, he didn't have all of it. Further, upon an appraisal, he found that his home was worth far less than he owed. Mr. Blue wanted to keep his house, but knew it wasn't wise financially under the current terms. Adding to the dilemma was the fact that he couldn't show income for fear of losing it in his divorce. Because of this, he couldn't qualify for a loan modification. So, he decided to litigate. Mr. Blue figured best case he would get principal reduction and keep the home, worst case he could buy some time to make arrangements. As the facts of the case were unfolding, it turned out he had some very powerful arguments – his lender had made some egregious errors. In light of that information, he decided to push hard and forget about simply attaining time in the home. His case was costly and extensive, appealed all the way to Federal Circuit Court. And in the end, he won. His case was settled and his mortgage principal was cut almost in half with a minimal interest rate, amortized over 30 years. Moral of the story: Persistence can pay off so don't give up.

Case Study #4: What do you do when foreclosure notices begin stacking up? Naturally you wait until the Sheriff Sale has been completed, the redemption period is over, and eviction papers are posted on your door – then call an attorney to undo it all. This is how I met Mr. Pink. To be honest, I still don't know exactly how he got in the position he was in. He hardly communicated with my staff and I as he could merely manage some broken English. He had no case worth representing, but was desperate for some time to get his affairs in order. So, we filed an answer to the complaint on his behalf. Lo and behold, Mr. Pink ends up receiving a settlement offer for a loan modification with principal reduction and his case is promptly dismissed. Sometimes there is no rhyme or reason in this industry.

Case Study #5: Mr. Yellow is a strange fellow. He's a nice guy, but his way of thinking is just a little different. Conspiracy was his mantra – "the man" was taking his home from him. It couldn't possibly have anything to do with his poor money management skills (he made a decent living and his housing costs were reasonable)… Anyway, based on the facts my attorneys informed him that he couldn't do much more than prevent the foreclosure for a period of time. He decided to proceed. And he lost, just like we told him he would. He urged us to file a motion for reconsideration, despite a rather harsh reminder that it would have no effect and his money would be better used in obtaining new housing. Mr. Yellow then asked if he could supplement the brief with a letter of his own "to explain his situation". The attorney assigned to his file indicated clearly that such an effort would be futile and possibly harmful. Mr. Yellow reluctantly concurred. Shortly thereafter, the hearing was held. Our counsel was motioned over by the judge who then proceeded to ask about a ridiculous, hand-written letter he had received from his client that morning. Dumbfounded, the lawyer could merely utter "I told him not to". The case was dismissed immediately with prejudice. Lesson: When you hire professionals, listen to them!

Case Study #6: Sometimes you just have to laugh. That's how I felt when I was informed of Ms. Purple, one of my peer's customers. Ms. Purple took out her mortgage at 26 years old, a typical time for a first home. Not so typical is a first home being a million dollar mansion. Ms. Purple was approved for this seven figure mortgage due to a $100,000 down payment. That makes sense, until you take into account that the $100,000 came from another loan that had no down payment earlier that same day! The loan was kept current for a short while and then defaulted. Litigation regarding the mortgage has been in process for several years and is still active at the time of this writing. This is the best example I've come across personally of both sides taking complete advantage of the system.

Case Study #7: Mr. Black came to my office with a modest request: get a lower interest rate on his HELOC loan. He had never missed a payment, but his rate was so high that his loan would never be paid off without paying extra principal each month, which he could not afford to do. As a foreclosure defense firm, we are normally the last resort. Rare is the individual that preemptively acts on a mortgage issue – for good reason. Mr. Black's lender adamantly refused to entertain any sort of modification without him defaulting on the loan first. Unfortunately for Mr. Black, he worked for the government and would not allow for a credit hit for fear of losing his clearance. It's a classic catch-22; can't afford to pay and can't afford to default. It's entirely counter-intuitive, but being responsible and attempting to get on top of the problem before it escalates is not allowed by most lenders.

Case Study #8: Mr. Orange is a wealthy man. He lives in a beautiful home on the water and works as a full-time investor. To him, when the housing market crashed, it was simply a matter of dollars and cents. His home wasn't worth what he owed so he decided to strategically foreclose. Mr. Orange came to us prior to missing a payment to ensure we protected his rights throughout. We succeeded in settling his HELOC for about $200,000 down to $20,000 which he paid in cash. As it stood, the junior lien holder wasn't going to receive a cent, so that was a win-win. Shortly thereafter, his home was sold at Sheriff's Sale – for drastically less than the amount he owed. Mr. Orange promptly redeemed this property and we were able to procure a waiver of deficiency on his behalf. The result: Mr. Orange owns his home free and clear and his property is no longer upside down. There are three important lessons to glean from his case. Junior liens can usually be reduced and that should always be attempted. Strategic foreclosure can be a wise decision. And redemption rights, when able to exercise them, are particularly advantageous to homeowners.

Case Study #9: Ms. Gray's father was in default in 2010. She worked with his lender on his behalf for a period of time – her father doesn't speak English. In 2011 she decided to hire my firm to assist as it was going beyond her expertise level. The case apparently had no merit, but all she wanted was maximum time so we agreed to help. To date, we have simply requested information and entertained various loan modification attempts. Her father is still in the home and it has still not gone to auction. What's the point? Information requests are powerful. Often they cannot be properly answered – and therefore foreclosure can't be lawfully initiated. Use them to your advantage.

Case Study #10: Mr. Red's union had been striking for an extended period of time and therefore his income had taken a severe hit. This put him in a position where it came down to food for his kids or mortgage payments – he chose the former. Mr. Red did not live beyond his usual means, choosing to live in very modest accommodations. His plan was to litigate against his lender to bide time until the strike ended and he could catch up on his payments. The strike didn't end like he thought it would and it seemed more and more likely that the home would ultimately be lost. When he was eventually ruled against, he elected to appeal. The bank saw this is a sign that he was a man of principal and would contest regardless of logic (his legal bills at that level would exceed his normal monthly payments). Further, he had legitimate issues of fact to argue. To avoid ongoing litigation costs, the bank offered Mr. Red a settlement whereby he would dismiss his case, vacate in 90 days, and in return receive $8,000. We advised him to accept, and he wisely took our advice. He had ample time to make arrangements and that sum amounted to about 20% of the value of his home. This stands as an exceptional example of when it is in the best interest of a homeowner to accept a "cash for keys" relocation agreement.

Case Study #11: I have a confession to make: I'm not proud of every case that my firm has been involved with. In our start-up phase, we took some work that today would be refused as they go against my personal beliefs. One stands out in particular. Mr. Green is wealthy as a result of inheritance, but in looking at his personal financial documents you'd never know that. He hired us to represent him regarding four different properties – each with tenants in them. His objective was to avoid paying mortgages but still collect rent. These properties already had positive cash flow on a monthly basis and only one had negative equity. We have since withdrawn from this matter as he didn't pay his bill to us either. This example has nothing to do with defending foreclosures or the housing market but makes an important point. Exploitation of the system does exist – and it does put a negative stigma on those who have legitimate issues to contest.

Case Study #12: Occasionally lenders are more than accommodating to homeowners. Such is the case with Ms. Brown. She came to my office in 2011, desiring a loan modification. She had previously been denied on her own and thought we might be able to help. Since then, she has had a half dozen loan modification offers, despite repeated denials and not making a payment since prior to my meeting her. Her house has not been sold at Sheriff's Sale as of this writing and her seventh attempt to modify is now currently under review. Ms. Brown will not be approved. Why? Because she has taken the money she saves each month by not paying her mortgage and allocated it to frivolous junk. I can't be more specific, because the expenses vary on a monthly basis, but somehow she manages to be left with zero or close to it every month. Ms. Brown makes a decent living, she's not experiencing hardship by any means. Despite numerous reminders to make sure her bank statements show that she can afford a modified mortgage, she refuses to adjust her spending – even though she had previously budgeted that amount each month for her mortgage. Moral of the story: Don't be the person that doesn't qualify for a modification because you have zero discipline with your money.

Case Study #13: I have to continue preaching the money management monologue. Some people have hardships – I understand that and empathize. Too many people simply lack any semblance of discipline though. One such couple stands out to me: the Violets. Both of them are highly educated and cumulatively they earn over $200,000 per year and have done so for some time. Their home was not extravagant, worth less than their annual income – a comfortable home to raise a family in a safe neighborhood. The Violets somehow managed to fall behind on their payments and entered into a Chapter 13 bankruptcy to attempt to save their home. At some point, their case was dismissed due to an error in procedure. I was not involved in their bankruptcy and therefore do not wish to disclose those details. Their home reverted to a foreclosure status and that's when I came in contact with the Violets. At this point, their best option was time, which we got them. Eventually eviction came and they moved into a rental home. Today they pay significantly more in rent per month than their house payment was. I still don't know how they managed to get into a foreclosure predicament in the first place. Or how they are able to pay their rent each month, but couldn't afford to pay for a house they owned. The Violets are a perfect example to all of what not to do. Take note and ensure that your expenses are kept in check – remember: it's not what you make, it's what you keep.

Case Study #14: Proper notification remains one of the big problems with foreclosures. Mr. Gold was a victim of such incompetency. The details of his foreclosure process are irrelevant to the point of this story. Suffice to say, his home was seized improperly and the bank was well aware of the errors.

Despite that, eviction commenced and he was force to relocate. Then, *after he had already moved,* he received notice that the Sheriff Sale had been rescinded. This is when he called my firm. We're in the process of litigating to obtain damages for Mr. Gold as his family was clearly harmed by blatant errors on the lender's part. Time will tell how this case pans out, but this scenario serves as a great illustration of how haphazard notification procedures are sometimes handled.

Case Study #15: Competent counsel is the best friend of a homeowner facing foreclosure. However, inept or negligent attorneys are not uncommon and they can have detrimental effects on a family in this position. One such incident involves the Bronze family. They knew their best chance of contesting was through a lawyer, so they hired one. The details of the case are unknown to me, but the end result was that their counsel entered into a consent judgment *unbeknownst to them.* What did that do? It only alleviated any rights they had and allowed for a voluntary relocation date in exchange for $2,000. One of my attorneys got a call from this couple when a Sheriff showed up at their door to remove them. The Sheriff was kind and gave them a temporary stay to figure out what happened when they explained their situation. Unfortunately, there was nothing we could do for these people. Judges loathe to overturn a consent order for obvious reasons. This is an extreme case of poor attorney practices, but is not as unusual as you might think. Make sure this doesn't happen to you. Always get several references prior to retaining counsel. And demand to see any offers that are presented from the opposing party.

Case Study #16: There's something to be said for just going for it. That's what Ms. Silver did, and it has worked out well for her. She came to me having already not paid on her mortgage in almost three years. Her goal was simple: maximum time in the home. She didn't think she had a chance at keeping it, so she decided to save money so that she'd be prepared when the time came to leave. I appreciated her realism, especially since the home had already been sold at auction and she was facing a District Court action for eviction. Due to the circumstances, the attorney on her file informed her that she should prepare for three to six months of time in the home. That was two years ago. She's still in the home and is now being considered for a loan modification. The attorneys I work with do a great job, and this was no exception, but the real credit goes to the opposing counsel and judge. The lawyer for Ms. Silver's bank was from out of state and clearly didn't pay much attention. Her judge was favorable to homeowners. You never know either of those things until you're involved in the courts. The point: Don't be afraid to stand up for yourself; you might be pleasantly surprised by the results.

Appendix F: Functional Glossary

Real estate, finance, and law, like most other professional industries, are plagued with jargon. For those involved with those subjects regularly, it makes things easier. For everyone else, it turns simple English into a cryptic code. Dictionary definitions often lead to even more confusion. I put in a great deal of effort to avoid complex verbiage in this book. When practicing the concepts you've learned, you'll not likely sidestep encounters with those literary monsters. No excuses – you must be prepared. Below are practical descriptions of many commonly used terms so nobody can confuse you with their lingo.

Acceleration: When a mortgage loan defaults, the lender has the right to demand full payment of the note. This is known as acceleration of the loan.

Administrative expenses: These are the fees incurred in a Chapter 13 bankruptcy – typically the trustee's fees and attorney's fees. Administrative costs usually account for about 10% of total payments under the plan.

Amortization: Paying off a loan with regular payments over a set period.

Annual percentage rate (APR): The interest rate on a loan on an annual basis. It's more accurate to look at the APR than the stated interest rate when calculating the cost of borrowing.

Appraisal: An expert's evaluation of what a property is worth currently.

Assignment: A document showing that ownership of a mortgage and the underlying promissory note have been transferred from the one owner to another.

Automatic stay: Filing for bankruptcy imposes an automatic injunction that prohibits most collection activities, including foreclosure, for a period of time.

Balloon payment: A large one-time payment due as the last payment on a loan.

Bankruptcy petition preparer: A non-lawyer who helps someone with bankruptcy. They cannot give legal advice or represent you in court.

Borrower: A person that received a loan.

Chapter 7 bankruptcy: A form of bankruptcy which liquidates the debtor's assets to pay creditors. Certain property is exempt and some debts cannot be discharged. Most liens (i.e. mortgages) survive even after discharge, though the debtor is no longer personally liable for payment.

Chapter 13 bankruptcy: A type of bankruptcy that reorganizes debts and the petitioner pays all or a portion of them over three to five years.

Chapter 13 plan: A document filed in a Chapter 13 bankruptcy that shows how all of the debtor's projected disposable income will be used to pay debts owed.

Closed-end loan: Any loan that must be paid off within a certain period of time (i.e. mortgage).

Collateral: Property pledged by a borrower as security for a loan. If the loan defaults, that property can be seized by the lender.

Complaint: A formal document that initiates a lawsuit.

Conventional loan: A mortgage loan issued to a borrower with good credit. These are not insured by the federal government.

Credit counseling: A brief course (~ 1 hour online) that consumers must attend prior to filing for bankruptcy.

Creditor: A person or institution to whom money is owed.

Creditors' meeting: A meeting at which bankruptcy trustees and creditors may question the filing debtor about property and debts.

Debtor: Someone who owes money to another person or business. This is also the term used for those filing for bankruptcy.

Deed in lieu: An arrangement under which homeowners can get out from under a mortgage and prevent a foreclosure, by signing the deed to their home over to the lender in exchange for the lender's agreement to not hold the homeowner liable for the remaining amount of the mortgage.

Deed of trust: In about half the states, a loan that is secured by real estate is termed a deed of trust. Deeds of trust are like mortgages, except that unlike mortgages, deeds of trust typically have a power of sale clause that lets the lender have the property sold at a public auction if the homeowner defaults on the payments (non-judicial foreclosure).

Default: Failing to meet the requirements of an agreement. For mortgages, this usually means missing three payments.

Deficiency: The amount a homeowner owes the lender after a house is sold at a foreclosure sale for less than the actual debt owed. Most states allow for the pursuit of a deficiency judgment.

Discharge: A court order issued at the conclusion of a bankruptcy case which legally relieves the debtor of personal liability for debts that can be discharged in that type of bankruptcy.

Equity: The amount of cash you would pocket if you sold your house and paid off all the liens. This is also a term used to describe the concept of fairness in the court room.

Exemptions (exempt property): Property and monetary amounts that a debtor is entitled to keep in a Chapter 7 bankruptcy.

Fannie Mae (Federal National Mortgage Association). A government-chartered corporation set up to purchase mortgages from original lenders to group and sell them to private investors.

Federal Housing Administration (FHA). A federal agency that insures first mortgage lenders against loss when a loan is made following FHA regulations.

Forbearance: A period of time, usually three to six months, in which a lender allows a homeowner to skip mortgage payments. This sum must be paid back later with increased payments or additional payments.

Foreclosure: The legal process by which a creditor satisfies a debt through the seizure of property to sell it. See "Judicial foreclosure" and "Non-judicial foreclosure."

Forgiven debt: Debt that is written off as uncollectable by the creditor. In the foreclosure context, a mortgage owner forgives debt when a foreclosure occurs and the property is sold for less than is owed on the mortgage (see "Short Sale"). Forgiven debts count as taxable income.

Freddie Mac (Federal Home Mortgage Corporation): Like Fannie Mae, a government-chartered company used to purchase mortgages from lenders to package and sell them to private investors.

Ginnie Mae (Government National Mortgage Corporation): A quasi-governmental agency that guarantees pools of FHA- and VA-insured loans that have been packaged into securities for investment purposes.

Home equity loan (HELOC): A loan made to a homeowner with equity in the house used for collateral. HELOC loans are secondary to first mortgages.

Injunction: A court order prohibiting a person or entity from taking specified actions.

Interest: Money paid regularly at a particular rate for the use of loaned funds.

Interest-only loan: A type of mortgage loan where the borrower makes payments only on the loan's interest for a limited period of time. The mortgage payments are much lower than they would be initially, but the overall amount of the loan increases (negative amortization). When the amount of the loan reaches a certain level, the borrower must begin making much higher payments to make up for the increase.

Insolvent: When a person's or business's assets are worth less than their liabilities.

Judicial foreclosure. A type of foreclosure in which the foreclosing party must file a lawsuit to seek a judgment allowing the property to be sold at auction.

Judicial lien: A lien created by recording a court money judgment against the debtor's property.

Lien: A legal claim against property that must be paid before title to the property can be transferred. Liens on real estate can also often be collected through foreclosure.

Lifting the stay: When a bankruptcy court allows a creditor to continue with debt collection or other activities that are otherwise banned by the automatic stay.

Lis Pendens: A formal notice of a pending legal action which clouds title of a property.

Loan term: The loan term is the period during which the loan is due to be repaid in full. Most mortgage loans have 15- or 30-year terms, though some are as long as 40 years.

Market value: The highest price one would pay and the lowest price the seller would accept on a property on the open market.

Mechanics' liens: Liens put on real estate when labor ordered for the house is not paid for.

Means test: A formula that uses predefined income and expense categories to determine whether a debtor should be allowed to file for Chapter 7 bankruptcy.

Mediation: A process that allows you, a representative from your mortgage company, and a neutral third party mediator to meet and discuss alternatives to foreclosure.

Modification: A process which alters a loan agreement in some way agreed upon by both mortgagor and mortgagee.

Mortgage servicer: A type of business that large mortgage owners hire to administer their mortgage portfolios. The mortgage servicer typically accepts and records mortgage payments, negotiates a workout in case of a default, and supervises the foreclosure process.

Mortgage: A contract in which a loan to buy real estate is secured by the property as collateral.

Mortgage-backed security (MBS): A type of investment backed by mortgage loans that have been packaged into pools or trusts, with payments on the underlying mortgages generating the return for investors.

Mortgagee: The lending party in a mortgage agreement.

Mortgagor: The borrowing party in a mortgage agreement.

Negative amortization: Negative amortization occurs when payments do not cover the amount of interest due for a loan period. This happens when low payments are combined with high interest rates.

Negative equity: Negative equity is when property's market value is less than the total owed on all the liens recorded against it. Popular terms for negative equity are "upside down" and "underwater".

Non-judicial foreclosure: A foreclosure that proceeds outside of court.

Notice to quit: A formal written notice given to the occupant of real estate indicating that they must vacate the property within a specified period of time or they will be forced out by a Sheriff.

Open-ended loan: A loan without a definite term or end date.

Originator: The entity that makes the loan for a homebuyer.

Predatory lending: Lending money under terms that are likely to cause a default in payments because the payments are too high compared to income level, or due to hidden fees and costs that are not properly disclosed.

Proof of service: A document signed under penalty of perjury by the person serving a document showing how the service was made, who made it, and when.

Real Estate Settlement Procedures Act (RESPA): A federal law designed to protect consumers from abusive practices in the residential real estate market.

Redemption right: The homeowner's right to buy back the house after a foreclosure sale by reimbursing the new owner the amount of the purchase price, plus interest and fees. This right is not available in every state.

Refinance: Using a new loan to pay off the current loan to get a better interest rate.

Reinstatement: Getting current on your mortgage by making up missed payments, plus interest and fees. Reinstatement cures loan default.

Rescission: The act of canceling a loan agreement or completed foreclosure and restoring borrower and lender to the positions they were in before the loan or foreclosure.

Reverse mortgage: A type of loan designed for people who are 62 or older and have considerable equity in their homes. The lender essentially buys the home and uses the equity to provide the homeowner with a set monthly payment over his or her life based on the amount of the equity in the home. At the owners' death, the lender takes possession of the property.

Second mortgage: A mortgage on property that is already mortgaged.

Secured creditor: The owner of a secured claim.

Secured debt: A debt secured by collateral.

Secured interest: A claim to property used as collateral.

Secured property: Property that is collateral for a secured debt.

Securitization: The process of converting a lender's ownership interest in an original mortgage into an investment vehicle that can be sold.

Short sale: A sale of a house that has negative equity. It must be approved by a lender because the sale won't entirely pay off the loan.

Subprime mortgage loan: A loan that carries a higher interest rate than a comparable loan because of the borrower's low credit rating.

Summary Disposition Motion: A document filed with the court to state that the other party has no legitimate issues of fact to argue and therefore the judge should dismiss that party.

Summons and complaint: Legal documents that are served on a homeowner to initiate a lawsuit. In regards to foreclosure, these documents commence judicial foreclosure or an eviction.

Tax lien: A statutory lien imposed on property to secure payment of back taxes.

Trustee: An official appointed by the bankruptcy court to carry out the administrative tasks associated with a bankruptcy.

Truth in Lending Act (TILA): A federal law that requires lenders to give borrowers standard disclosures of the cost and payment terms of the loan.

Appendix G: Suggested Reading

One of the best books to learn more about the Federal Reserve that I highly recommend to all is *The Creature from Jekyll Island* by G. Edward Griffin.

There are too many books to list on the current economic state of the United States, and particularly related to the housing market, but a few suggestions include:

- *Too Big to Fail* by Andrew Ross Sorkin
- *Meltdown* by Thomas E. Woods and Ron Paul
- *Who Stole the American Dream?* by Hedrick Smith

A half dozen of the best books on proper money management and personal finance that I'd recommend to all includes:

- *The Richest Man in Babylon* by George Clason
- *Secrets of the Millionaire Mind* by T. Harv Eker
- *The Millionaire Next Door* by Thomas J. Stanley
- *Rich Dad, Poor Dad* by Robert Kiyosaki
- *The Science of Being Rich* by Wallace Wattle
- *Think and Grow Rich* by Napoleon Hill.

Of course, there are many more available, but these are tried and true.

Eminent Domain: How to use eminent domain to stop foreclosures, rescue homeowners and save communities by Michael Sauvante and Vari MacNeil, mentioned in Part 4, is a fantastic resource for those looking to learn more about this topic. Various works from Robert Hockett on eminent domain are quite informative as well.

There aren't many good books available for homeowners looking to defend themselves against foreclosure – that's why I wrote this book. One does stand out as a source I would encourage you to check out for a different perspective on the topic is *The Foreclosure Survival Guide* by Stephen Elias. Mr. Elias was a great author on many topics regarding legal and financial matters and was also a part of the Nolo.com team which is an amazing, free resource available to all.

Complete Bibliography

1 "United States Census Bureau: Historical Census of Housing Table", https://www.census.gov/hhes/www/housing/census/historic/owner.html, (January 7, 2014)

2 "Wikipedia: Executive Order 6102", http://en.wikipedia.org/wiki/Executive_Order_6102, (January 8, 2014)

3 "U.S. Department of State: Office of the Historian", http://history.state.gov/milestones/1969-1976/nixon-shock, (January 8, 2014)

4 "Cornell University Law School Legal Information Institute: 12 U.S. Code § 1841 – Definitions", http://www.law.cornell.edu/uscode/text/12/1841, (January 10, 2014)

5 "Wikipedia: Paul Volker", http://en.wikipedia.org/wiki/Paul_Volcker#Chairman_of_the_Federal_Reserve, (January 11, 2014)

6 "Public Citizen: Blind Faith: How Deregulation and Enron's Influence Over Government Looted Billions from Americans", http://www.citizen.org/cmep/article_redirect.cfm?ID=7104, (January 13, 2014)

7 "PBS Frontline: Wendy Gramm", http://www.pbs.org/wgbh/pages/frontline/president/players/gramm.html, (January 13, 2014)

8 "Wikipedia: Citigroup", http://en.wikipedia.org/wiki/Citigroup, (January 13, 2014)

9 “Wikipedia: Gramm-Leach-Bliley Act”, http://en.wikipedia.org/wiki/Gramm%E2%80%93Leach%E2%80%93Bliley_Act, (January 13, 2014)

10 “Wikipedia: Causes of the United States Housing Bubble”, http://en.wikipedia.org/wiki/Causes_of_the_United_States_housing_bubble#cite_note-14, (January 13, 2014)

11 Lisa Rerer, “McCain guru linked to subprime crisis”, http://www.politico.com/news/stories/0308/9246.html, (January 13, 2014)

12 Terry Frieden, “FBI warns of mortgage fraud 'epidemic'”, http://www.cnn.com/2004/LAW/09/17/mortgage.fraud/, (January 13, 2014)

13 David B. Grusky, Bruce Western, Christopher Wimer, *The Great Recession* (Russell Sage Foundation, 2011), 33-34

14 “Wikipedia: Subprime Mortgage Crisis”, http://en.wikipedia.org/wiki/Subprime_mortgage_crisis#Homeowner_speculation (January 15, 2014)

15 “Wikipedia: Credit Default Swaps”, http://en.wikipedia.org/wiki/Credit_default_swap (January 15, 2014)

16 Sorkin, Andrew, "JP Morgan Pays $2 a Share for Bear Stearns", http://www.nytimes.com/2008/03/17/business/17bear.html?pagewanted=all (January 15, 2014)

17 James R. Barth, Tong Li, Wenling Lu, Triphon Phumiwasana, Glenn Yago, *The Rise and Fall of the U.S. Mortgage and Credit Markets* (Milkin Institute, 2009), *i*

18 “Russell Sage Foundation: Real Mean and Median Income, Families and Individuals”, http://www.russellsage.org/sites/all/files/chartbook/Income%20and%20Earnings.pdf (January 17, 2014)

19 “United States Census Bureau: Census of Housing”, https://www.census.gov/hhes/www/housing/census/historic/values.html (January 17, 2014)

20 Van Voorhis, Scott, “Homeowners Who Strategically Default”, http://www.boston.com/realestate/news/blogs/renow/2009/09/homeowners_who.html (January 20, 2014)

21 Ben Hallman, “Mortgage Settlement Report Finds Banks Reluctant To Reduce Principal, Despite Promises”, http://www.huffingtonpost.com/2013/02/21/mortgage-settlement-report_n_2736093.html (January 24, 2014)

22 Alan Zibel, “Home Loan Modifications: Only A Fraction Of Eligible Homeowners Have Been Helped”, http://www.huffingtonpost.com/2009/08/04/home-loan-modifications-o_n_250797.html (January 24, 2014)

23 Alejandro Lazo, “Foreclosure rate slows as repossession timeline lengthens”, http://articles.latimes.com/2011/may/12/business/la-fi-foreclosures-20110512 (January 27, 2014)

24 “Realty Trac: U.S. REAL ESTATE STATISTICS & FORECLOSURE TRENDS SUMMARY”, http://www.realtytrac.com/statsandtrends (February 2, 2014)

25 “The World Bank: Bank capital to assets ratio (%)”, http://data.worldbank.org/indicator/FB.BNK.CAPA.ZS (February 3, 2014)

26 “United States Census Bureau: USA Counties”, http://censtats.census.gov/usa/usa.shtml (February 3, 2014)

27 “U.S. Debt Clock: North Dakota”, http://www.usdebtclock.org/state-debt-clocks/state-of-north-dakota-debt-clock.html (February 4, 2014)

28 "Core Logic: National Foreclosure Report", http://www.corelogic.com/research/foreclosure-report/national-foreclosure-report-april-2013.pdf (February 4, 2014)

29 "Bureau of Labor Statistics: Unemployment Rates for States", http://www.bls.gov/web/laus/laumstrk.htm (February 4, 2014)

30 Michael B. Sauter, Thomas C. Frohlich, Alexander E.M. Hess, Ashley Allen, "Best- and worst-run states: Survey of all 50", http://www.usatoday.com/story/money/business/2013/11/22/best-worst-run-states/3671359/ (February 4, 2014)

31 Ellen Brown, "North Dakota's Economic "Miracle"—It's Not Oil", http://www.yesmagazine.org/new-economy/the-north-dakota-miracle-not-all-about-oil (February 4, 2014)

32 Ellen Brown, "A Choice for States: Banks, Not Budget Crises", http://www.yesmagazine.org/new-economy/a-choice-for-states-banks-not-budget-crises (February 4, 2014)

33 "U.S. Debt Clock: National Debt Clock", http://www.usdebtclock.org/ (February 5, 2014)

About the Author

David Prentice is from the metro-Detroit area - one of the hardest hit regions of the United States with regards to the housing market crash. Since 2010 he has owned and operated Home Team, a law practice solely dedicated to assisting homeowners with foreclosure defense. Over the past three years he's also opened and managed Partners Recovery Solutions, a firm focused on helping families with distressed real estate issues utilizing other avenues outside of the legal system. Most recently, he has begun to get involved with local politics in an effort to revamp the economic status of his community. His ventures revolve around his passion for educating people using his modest, practical style.

Made in the USA
Monee, IL
08 November 2026

67386975R10111